FRIENDSHIP

FRIENDSHIP

HANDLE WITH CARE

FROM:

Jane McWhorter

GOSPEL ADVOCATE COMPANY
P.O. BOX 150
NASHVILLE, TENNESSEE 37202

Published by Gospel Advocate Co.
P.O. Box 150, Nashville, TN 37202
http://www.gospeladvocate.com

ISBN 0-89225-383-5

Dedicated to all the friends who have graced my
own pathway of life

Table of Contents

HANDLE WITH CARE

The Blessings of Friendship

The passing of time brings its own wisdom. Youth tends to take friends for granted, but the mature years have a way of bringing the important values of life into sharper focus. Then we realize the blessings of true friendship.

The Christian takes God at His word and goes through life scattering the seeds of friendship that are taught in the Scriptures. We obey these precepts, not simply because we desire the joys of friendship but primarily because we want to obey God and trust that He knows what is best.

When these seeds fall into receptive hearts, friendships will spring up along the pathway of life. Each friendship is unique. Some are like roses, but others are like lilies, daffodils, violets or beautiful wildflowers. Each, in its own way, brings a special blessing to our lives.

The garden of friendship requires careful cultivation and should never be taken for granted. We must be on constant guard for the weeds that always are lurking beneath the surface with the potential for choking the tender plants.

This study has flooded my mind with memories of so many people who have been a part of my own journey along the pathway of life. It has been said that we are composed of bits and pieces of everyone who has ever crossed our path. I am eternally grateful for each one and the impact all have had on my life.

CHAPTER 1

What Is a Friend?

"The most I can do for my friend is simply to be his friend."
— Henry David Thoreau

To most of us, the mere mention of the word "friend" brings a warm feeling. We all need friends in times of troubles and in moments of joy. Many years ago Cicero stated this principle so clearly: "Friendship adds a brighter radiance to prosperity and lightens the burden of adversity by dividing and sharing it."

Which of us knows the strength we have gained from the touch of a dear friend during troubled times? We also remember the deep joy we received when we had someone special to share with us a moment of great happiness.

A life without friends is indeed a lonely one. Babies who are deprived of love and affection soon physically waste away. Prisoners of war have little chance of survival when they are kept in isolation for long periods of time. Studies have shown that most lonely people have shorter life spans and more psychosomatic illnesses than people who are surrounded by friends.

We can be in the midst of hundreds of people and yet be lonely. Most of us have been in crowds without a familiar face, and we have felt completely alone. Today's mobile society, with its frequent moves and frantic pace of life, is not as conducive to the de-

velopment of friendships as was the community of bygone years
with its barn-raisings, quilting bees, church socials, and the interaction of everyone in the area.

Benefits of Friendships

"What I really value is neither fame, fortune, nor genius, but
loving and being loved." — Victor Hugo

So much of our time is spent in acquiring things. We build elab-
orate houses and furnish them exquisitely. We buy fashionable clothes,
luxury cars, and other expensive adult toys. Then we invest years of
our lives in the upkeep of these things. We clean. We polish. We repair. We devote many working hours to have the money to purchase
insurance to protect these things in the event that they are stolen or
damaged by fire.

In the process of acquiring all these items, we can easily neglect
the building of friendships and may one day find ourselves very lonely people who have allowed materialism to build a wall between ourselves and our friends. Sometimes we get to the end of life and realize that we have neglected one of the most priceless treasures we
ever could have — good friends.

The benefits of friendships are myriad.

Friends give us roots. We all need to belong and feel a connection with people. When we are perplexed, having someone to whom
we can turn for encouragement is such a stabilizing influence. Gone
are the days when people grew up in one community and spent the
remainder of their lives there, surrounded by caring relatives and
friends to whom they could turn. As people move from one job to
another in different parts of the country, more and more they are
feeling the deprivations of rootlessness.

Friends give us loving acceptance. How wonderful it is to know
that we have certain people in our lives who accept us with all our
peculiarities and love us anyway. No one can be complete emotionally without this kind of assurance.

"The greatest happiness of life is the conviction that we are loved, loved for ourselves, or rather loved in spite of ourselves."
— Victor Hugo

Friends help us bear our burdens. A friend is there to share the load when we cannot bear it alone. The wise writer of Ecclesiastes penned these words: "Two are better than one; because they have a good reward for their labor. For if they fall, the one will lift up his fellow: but woe to him that is alone when he falleth; for he hath not another to help him up" (Ecclesiastes 4:9-10).

Sometimes the only help we need is a listening ear and an encouraging word as we vocalize our frustrations and seek solutions. Talking about a problem with a trusted friend helps to keep our perspectives straight and puts suffering into its proper context.

A number of years ago, our family was involved in a head-on collision that necessitated nearly a year of physical recovery for me and an even longer period of emotional adjustment to a crushed face. I could not have worked my way through my own questions of why without friends. My own searching found answers as I tearfully wrote *Let This Cup Pass*. Since that time, many people have come to me with well-worn copies of the book and have expressed gratitude for the strength they found in its pages. I am thankful that I could stand by them vicariously and offer help just as people have given me the strength to get up and try again.

Friends help to complete that which is lacking in our own personalities. Have you ever noticed how often opposites seem to attract, especially in marriage? The always punctual one usually finds companionship with someone who is habitually tardy. The neat person is attracted to one who rarely puts things away. If we could only recognize this oddity as something that results from a basic longing for whatever is lacking in our own lives, we could be spared many heartaches.

Friends can help us grow spiritually. How wonderful it is to have a close friend who can offer encouragement as well as act as a mirror to our souls and enable us to realize mistakes that should be corrected. What a blessing to have someone who gently can help us gain a sense of perspective and see our areas of weakness. "Faithful are the wounds of a friend" (Proverbs 27:6). "Iron sharpeneth iron; so a man sharpeneth the countenance of his friend" (Proverbs 27:17).

Friends heighten our joys by being there in times of happiness. How empty it is to receive some sort of honor and have no one to share the joy with us in that moment of exaltation. When our loved ones are the recipients of an award, we long to find someone to share in our happiness.

> "Grief can take care of itself, but to get the full value of a joy, you must have someone to divide it with." — Mark Twain

> "If a man could mount to Heaven and survey the mighty universe, his admiration of its beauties would be much diminished unless he had someone to share in his pleasure." — Cicero

Friends provide an opportunity for us to be the givers of the benefits of companionship. Our thinking becomes warped when we dwell only on the ways in which friends benefit us. Friendship is a two-way street. Our friends sustain us in so many different ways; we, in turn, reciprocate by being there for them in their good times and bad. When we minister to the needs of people, we ourselves become better people. To love and be loved is one of the greatest joys of life.

> "So long as we love, we serve. So long as we are loved by others, I would almost say we are indispensable; and no man is useless while he has a friend." — Robert Louis Stevenson

An even better reason for serving others was given by our Lord hundreds of years ago: "Inasmuch as ye have done it unto one of the least of these my brethren, ye have done it unto me" (Matthew 25:40).

Circles of Friendship

How many times have we read that a person is fortunate indeed if she has three or four friends in a lifetime? True, our best friends, who continue to be by our side throughout the years, are dear and few in number. However, to restrict the word "friend" to those individuals may cause us to overlook so many valuable people who play a significant part in our lives. Just as a rainbow is enhanced by its many different hues of color, so are our lives enriched by friendships in varying levels of development.

Acquaintances. We are surrounded by a large circle of people whom we will call "acquaintances." Within this group we would find former classmates, people with whom we daily come in contact in the business world, most of our neighbors, many people at church services, the cashier at the local grocery store, club members — anyone we know by name who has played a regular part in our lives in the course of daily living. We should remember that our dearest friends were, at one time or another, found within this large circle of acquaintances. These people should not be neglected because some of them undoubtedly have the potential for one day becoming our best friends.

Casual Friends. We may come in regular contact with many people, but we seem to gravitate toward some while we hold others at arm's length. Something about the chemistry of personalities bonds some people and yet causes the rejection of others. Within this realm we find our closer circle of friends at church services, some neighbors, some relatives whom we see only occasionally, the parents of our children's friends with whom we talk at ball games and other activities, and people with whom we work on various committees and projects and with whom our friendship cools when the activity is finished. Our lives are enriched by these casual friendships, but we are the losers if our relationships never develop more deeply than this level. Some people have outgoing personalities, which enable them to have a wide circle of casual friends; yet, such individuals are deprived emotionally if they never experience closer relationships.

Close Friends. In our circle of casual friends, we are attracted to some people more than others. Within this group we would find couples with whom we share meals in our homes or vacation time together, individuals who regularly engage in sporting events with us, people in the business world who often are our companions for lunch, or a neighbor who drops by frequently for a cup of coffee.

Best Friends. In the midst of our close friends, we find the few whom we could term "best friends." The number could vary from one to five or six. These friends are the ones to whom we immediately turn in times of trouble. When something wonderful happens to us, we reach for the telephone and share the news with our best friends before we tell anyone else. We feel comfortable when we are around these people and so secure in being accepted that we are willing to risk exposing our fears, our anxieties, our hopes and our dreams. We may see these people on a daily basis, or distance may separate us to the extent that our paths seldom cross. However, they have become so much a part of our lives that we never feel very far from them emotionally. With such people, we can pick up the threads of friendship whenever we meet and feel that we have never been apart.

All the people in these four circles of friendship have something to contribute to our lives; we, in turn, have qualities to offer for their enrichment. We may not think a person in one of the outer circles has the characteristics necessary for one day becoming a best friend, but our lives may be made better if we only will crack the doors of our hearts and allow another person to come in. We could be delightfully surprised.

Definition of a Friend

Giving a concise definition of the word "friend" is difficult. We bring our own backgrounds, our experiences, and even our stages in life to the definition. Each of us probably would have given a different explanation 20 years ago.

We are much like the blind men who touched different parts of an elephant and tried to describe the animal. The one who felt the tail thought the elephant was like a rope. Touching the trunk made another man think the animal was like a snake. The man who felt the massive side of the creature surmised that it was like a wall. The one who encountered the leg believed the beast was like a tree trunk. The ear reminded another man of a large fan. And on the story goes.

Trying to define "friend" is just about as difficult as stating the meanings of the word "love" or "beauty." Ask a hundred people, and you undoubtedly will receive a hundred different answers because much is in the eye of the beholder. The mystical quality defies description because friendship is an emotion.

A story is told about an English publication in which was offered a prize for the best definition of "friend." Among the thousands of answers received were these:

One who multiplies joys and divides grief;

One who understands our silence;

A volume of sympathy bound in cloth; and

A watch that beats true for all time and never runs down.

The winning definition: "A friend is the one who comes in when the whole world has gone out."

Poets and sages throughout the years have offered their own definitions:

"Friends are a single soul inhabiting two bodies." — Aristotle

"Friendship is a sheltering tree." — Samuel Taylor Coleridge

"A friend is a present you give yourself." — Robert Louis Stevenson

"A friend is, as it were, a second self." — Cicero

"A friend is a person with whom I may be sincere. Before him, I may think aloud." — Ralph Waldo Emerson

In my pilot study of the subject of friendship, a class of women gave their definitions of "friend." They answered that a friend is someone who understands your feelings, likes you for what you are, makes you feel comfortable when you are around them, allows you to be yourself, is trustworthy, will do what you ask of her and will not make you feel that you are imposing, sympathizes with you, is worthy of your confidence, shares joys and sorrows, is there for you no matter what, accepts you despite your faults, and makes you feel safe in baring your soul. They said a friend is there regardless of years and distance, loves you in good and bad times, will not forsake you, is friendly, will never do you harm, can pick up where you left off no matter how much time and distance may separate the two of you, is open-minded, is dependable, is honest and will tell you the truth, is a good listener and will not judge, helps you be your best, defends you to other people, and will give you the benefit of a doubt.

The word "friend" may be difficult to define, but Proverbs 17:17 states that a friend loves at all times. The word "love" is also nebulous, but Paul shed light on its meaning when he described love in 1 Corinthians 13. In this passage he states that love is patient and kind, is never envious, is never selfish or rude, is not irritable or touchy, does not hold grudges, rejoices when truth is victorious, can endure anything, trusts to the end, and never gives up hope.

We could substitute the word "friend" for love and have a wonderful description.

It has been said that friendship is a bond between two faulty people who can encourage one another to be better in spite of their shortcomings.

It is difficult to understand the exact reason for bonding in friendship. The individuals' common interests, their emotional chemistry, their goals in life, their personalities, and their needs for one another attract them and cement their hearts to stand by each other through both the good and the troubled times of life. We may look at two of our acquaintances who are close friends and wonder what attracted them to one another, but there is something about the emotional make-up that draws them together and makes them right for one another.

> "If anyone should ask me to give a reason why I loved my friend, there could be only one answer: 'Because he was he, because I was I.'" — Montaigne

Clarifying a Definition

Perhaps we can better understand the true meaning of the word "friend" if we leave the abstract words and put flesh and blood on the definition. We may not be able to write a meaning, but we all know what we are talking about when we mention the word.

Think back over the many friends you have had in the past. Take a stroll with me down memory lane as you put your own names and faces in these scenarios.

Do you remember your very first friend? I remember mine. Her name was Shirley Gray, and she lived down the street from me. We were best friends through the third grade, but then she moved away. I have not seen Shirley since that time. Should I say she was not my friend because I have had no contact with her for decades? Of course not! She had an impact upon me and made me a better person for having known her.

Can you remember your close friends through elementary school? You played ball with them and went to parties. Try to recall the ones who were closest to you.

How about high school? Can you remember the good times you had? Your circle of friends probably was wide at that time, but to which ones do you feel closest now? Do you still keep in touch with any of them? Have you exerted any effort to fan the fires of those friendships? Are certain people still dear to you? How do you feel when you receive a letter or phone call from one of them? Do you ever call or write?

What about your college friends? Life in the dorm is conducive to bonding as people are thrown together nearly 24 hours a day. Recall the names of the ones who were closest to you during that part of your life. Think back over the good times you had.

Do you remember the first "couple friends" you and your mate had in the early years of your marriage? No one had much by way of material wealth, but you had a good time together.

I never recopy a recipe. My cookbooks are filled with recipes from friends in years gone by. Some are scrawled on scraps of paper, on napkins, and even on pieces of paper plates. Wherever I happened to be with friends (homes, church dinners, etc.) and found a good dish, I wrote the recipe on whatever paper was available, along with the name of the person who shared her culinary secrets. Looking through my recipe books always brings back many memories, and I can still visualize the place and the people who were there.

Think back over the troubled times in your life. Which friends were there? I will never forget the people who waited by the side of my family in the intensive care unit of the hospital for long periods of time, even sleeping on the floor, just so my loved ones would not have to bear bad news alone. I remember who brought food for my family to eat, cared for my children, and did whatever they could to make our burdens lighter.

I well remember being called out of town for a crisis in our family. On our return trip, I told my husband I thought I would be all right if only I could make it back home and feel the arms of friends around me once again. What a strong bond we feel with our fellow Christians!

On and on we could go down the paths of our memories. I hope I have stimulated your thinking as you have recalled the people who have been dear to you through the years.

The Ebb and Flow of Friendships

"I am a part of all that I have met." — Alfred Lord Tennyson

As you have been reading through this part of the chapter, no doubt you have remembered people whom you had not thought about in a long time. Once many of the friendships were intense. These people were your best friends during some particular periods of your life. Some of them are no longer even in your address book. Does this mean those people are no longer your friends?

We must remember that friendships come and go. We have to allow for the normal ebb and flow of friends. We move to a different location and lose touch. Nothing went wrong with the relationships; distance simply was a factor against them. We ourselves are changing constantly. The qualities that appeal to us in a friend fluctuate as we change. The characteristics a more mature person looks for in friendship possibly are different from those a teenager is seeking.

The people who once were intensely close friends are still with us because we always carry in our hearts a part of everyone who has been dear to us. Our lives have touched, and because of the loving memories we are better people. Our relationship with them may have been casual or intense. Our initial contact may have been last week or 40 years ago. Through their love, they may have brought much joy to our lives, and we cherish their memories as we resolve to offer the same kind of love to other people. Perhaps they hurt us deeply. Instead of becoming bitter, we can be made better by promising never to hurt anyone in the same manner as we have been wounded. But we carry with us a part of everyone we have known as long as we live.

> "With the death of every friend I love, a part of me has been buried, but their contribution to my being of happiness, strength, and understanding remains to sustain me in an altered world."
> — Helen Keller

Layer upon layer, our hearts are thus composed of the influence other people have had in our lives. Some friendships were transitory, but they were an important part of our beings at that particular time. Remembering them is as refreshing as a warm breeze on a spring day. These friends are precious and should never be forgotten.

Other people fall into the category of "forever friends." These relationships developed at various stages along the trail of life and have weathered the test of time and distance. A special bonding has held us together for years. We may not see one another very often or write and phone as we would like, but a closeness between us is there. Some of our present friendships will fade away while others will become friends of the heart. All friends are blessings to our lives.

> "The comfort of having a friend may be taken away, but not that of having had one." — Seneca

Differences in the Friendships of Men and Women

Although it is indeed difficult for women to come to an agreement on a suitable definition of friendship, the problem is compounded even more when we interject the definitions given by men. Males and females are usually poles apart when each group discusses the subject.

One seldom hears of men who gather to study ways to improve their friendships or who study books relating to methods of deepening the marriage relationship (although there are a few). Most men do not think they need help in the area of relationships any more than they need assistance in asking for directions while on the road. To ask for help would be tantamount to admitting a weakness.

"Secret sisters" are quite common among women, but one never hears of "secret brothers." The commercial greeting card companies would become bankrupt if they depended upon men to purchase cards, especially those pertaining to the joys of friendship.

Childhood Beginnings

Little boys' friends usually develop from within the circle of an activity. Instead of having a best friend, most boys will call any teammate a friend. The circle of friends changes with whatever game is being played at that particular time. One more person's joining the group presents no problems. Boys have group secrets rather than one-to-one confidences.

Little boys bond at an early age through aggression and confrontation. As a schoolteacher, many times I have reprimanded two boys for fighting on the playground only to hear, "Aw, Teacher, he's my friend. We were just playing!"

Even at a tender age, girls exhibit significant differences in their friendship preferences. Whereas each person on a team is usually a little boy's friend, young girls tend to have smaller clusters of friends, and the friendships are decidedly more intense. A little girl without a best friend is rare indeed. During many years of teaching first-graders, I have tried to comfort numerous girls who were in tears because "Susie is my best friend, and she said she isn't going to play with me at recess!" The boys never seemed to care who their playmates were; one fellow was just as good as another.

Little girls have a more intense need for friendship than little boys do and are even more expressive as they show affection by holding hands, hugging, and passing notes that confirm their friendships. On the negative side, girls usually are more cruel than boys. Even young females tend to gossip and exclude other girls from the small-group situation.

Maturing with Age

Childhood friendship preferences tend to become even more pronounced as young boys and girls mature into adult men and women. Men still gravitate toward group friends rather than toward individual friendships. In fact, men often feel uncomfortable around one another unless they are engaging in an activity. Men bond by doing something together, especially as they meet adversity or danger. Strong masculine ties may be found in the loyalty and trust of the wartime combat unit or in the team spirit of fighting against the foe in sports.

Ask a man for his definition of a friend, and he typically will respond with: "A friend is someone I _____ with." The blank could be filled with any number of appropriate activities: work, hunt, fish, play ball, bowl, etc. The key is comradeship. The high-school locker room has been replaced by the battlefield of war, the place of business, the hunting lodge, the bowling alley, the tennis court, the ball field, or even the local restaurant where men congregate for morning coffee and the telling of stories.

The conversations of men normally revolve around things and happenings rather than personal feelings. Information is shared on a wide range of topics: cars, the business world, politics, sports, computers, hunting, fishing, current events, and other mutual interests.

The competitive spirit of the young boy on a ball team evolves into adult competitiveness and the natural desire for masculine superiority. Often it is seen in the form of bantering, as stories are told with an attitude of "Can you top this one?" whether it be the biggest fish caught or the tallest tale that can be told. Men need the approval of other men and characteristically seek it by a display of masculinity and competence.

Early in life, males are discouraged from touching one another except for the body contact in aggressive sports. The high fives and hugs of the spontaneous celebrations in a locker room after a game are subdued into the accepted handshake between men.

By way of summary, we may say that men tend to gravitate toward group friends as they jointly engage in an activity. Their conversations center around things (athletic competitions, cars, current events, and the business world) rather than their feelings and the emotional problems of other people. A man usually does not confide his feelings to a best friend. If he confides his true feelings to anyone at all, it is usually to one woman.

Women, on the other hand, are completely different from men in their friendship characteristics. Rather than having group friends, women tend to seek women with whom they can share confidences and feelings because they want to connect emotionally. Women also tend to have more friendships than a man.

Women want rather large webs of relationships for comfort and support, and yet a woman without a best friend is a very lonely person. She turns to her friends in time of joy and in times of trouble.

Because a woman usually is more verbal than a man, she finds it easier to express her true feelings. She often can withstand a rather severe emotional blow, such as the death of her husband or a divorce, more easily than most men because she is able to let her troubles flow through her as she confides in friends instead of allowing her problems to become bottled up inside.

Openness promotes connection with other people. Most women can tell their personal feelings even to casual female acquaintances. Because women do not generally receive emotional support from men, they depend upon other women. Not only are women aware of their own emotions, but they also are sensitive to the feelings of other people. A great deal of joking has been done concerning a woman's intuition, but much of her intuitiveness is a natural result of watching the other person's facial expressions and listening to the tone of voice. She is better able than a man to read between the lines and get to the heart of the real meaning of someone's words. She knows how to listen, how to ask questions, and how to draw feelings from people.

As caregivers, women have a deep interest in people and their feelings. They are nurturers as they travel through life and naturally encourage people with smiles, words of praise, small gifts, and notes of encouragement.

Women, much more than men, feel freer to touch. Adult men seldom go beyond a handshake, but most women are not at all uncomfortable in showing affection by means of hugs with one another.

In view of the vast differences in the friendships of men and those of women, it is small wonder that each group would probably give a different definition of the word "friend."

One important principle to remember is this: Men are satisfied with their definitions of friendship, and women are happy with theirs. Neither one is better than the other. Men and women are just different in their expectations. One group cannot change the other. We merely try to understand the differences and accept one another as we are.

Questions

1. Discuss the differences in the pace of life 100 years ago and today. How has today's culture been instrumental in promoting a feeling of isolation in people?
2. Why do we need roots? How can friends help us feel that we belong?
3. Friends give us loving acceptance. Does this mean that we never try to make other people aware of undesirable qualities in their lives? How far should acceptance go?
4. Discuss Ecclesiastes 4:9-10. Ask each class member to share a troubled time when friends were especially helpful.
5. Do you think that opposites often attract? How can this trait be beneficial? How can it be harmful?
6. Share examples of friends who have encouraged you in developing spiritual growth. How have they accomplished this? Include Proverbs 27:6, 17 in the discussion.
7. Why do we need someone to share in our happiness? Is this more important than sharing in times of trouble?
8. Why is it vital that we be the givers a fair amount of the time in a relationship? How do we benefit from giving?
9. According to Matthew 25:40, what is the ultimate purpose in serving people? How does this realization cause giving to become even more meaningful?

10. Discuss these four circles of friends, and give the characteristics of each: acquaintances, casual friends, close friends and best friends.

11. Ask each member of the class to write her own definition of "friend" on a slip of paper. Share these with the class. Compare them with the ones listed in this chapter. Were any of them alike? Why is it so difficult to define the word "friend"?

12. Substitute the word "friend" for the word "love" found in 1 Corinthians 13:4-8.

13. Why do we seem to bond with certain people in friendships?

14. When the word "friend" is mentioned, most people can associate a face with the word when it is difficult to give a verbal definition. Walk down the path of memory by discussing people who have been your friends during different times in your life.

15. Why is it natural for friendships to come and go during various times of our lives? Do you agree that we are composed of parts of every person who has ever crossed our paths?

16. Why do some people become forever friends and remain close to us in our hearts throughout a lifetime?

17. How do men and women differ in their concepts of friendship? Do you think this difference is good or bad? Why is understanding important in a friendship, especially in a marriage?

CHAPTER 2

Our Friendship with God

When people are asked about their friendship with God, they customarily respond with several different answers. To some, God is viewed as a majestic deity upon a throne, resplendent with glory and evoking only awe and reverence from His subjects.

Other people see Jehovah in the role of a policeman, who constantly watches our every move in an attempt to catch human beings in some sort of wrongdoing that would lead to eternal punishment.

To some people, familiarity is the tone underlying their relationship with the Father. In their concept, the phrase "the man upstairs" depicts their friendship with God as they endeavor to place the Almighty on the same plane of friendship as a next-door neighbor.

Still others seem to look upon God as a glorified servant, who always stands in readiness, waiting to deliver whatever requests might be made of Him.

Dare we claim to be friends with someone who is so majestic and who has the power to cast us into eternal punishment? Can we ever think of Him as our daily companion? Would calling Him our friend be sacrilegious?

In the Beginning

Human minds simply cannot comprehend the power of the Almighty, who could speak the world into being. After relating the events of His majestic creation, the inspired writer of Genesis records a seldom-mentioned, but important, event in the Scriptures.

After Adam and Eve had sinned by partaking of the forbidden fruit, their eyes were opened as they suddenly realized they were naked. When they sewed fig leaves together for a covering, the first inhabitants of the earth hid themselves among the trees in the garden. At this time "they heard the voice of the Lord God walking in the garden in the cool of the day" (Genesis 3:8). One is made to wonder if perhaps it had been a previous habit for them to walk and talk with God at the end of the day when the temperature cooled. If so, what a wonderful experience that must have been and how sad that sin marred such a close relationship!

Early Communication Between God and Man

Beginning with Adam, God talked with the head of each chosen family as He made His wishes known directly to the patriarchs. The divine account continues with God's talking to Cain and His instructions to Noah as well as to such men as Moses before the Law was given. The people had no way of knowing what God expected of them until His voice fell on their ears.

Imagine the awe these men must have felt as the Father made His wishes known. Try to visualize the reaction of Moses as he approached the bush that was burning and yet was not consumed. Commanded to remove his shoes since the ground was holy, Moses hid his face because he was afraid to look upon God (Exodus 3:6). Exodus 33:11 states that when the cloudy pillar descended upon the tabernacle, "the Lord spake unto Moses face to face, as a man speaketh unto his friend." The meaning of this verse must be interpreted in view of verse 20: "Thou canst not see my face: for there shall no man see me, and live." Evidently, the words of verse 11— "as a man speaketh unto his friend"— must have been a figurative description of the conversation between Moses and the Lord, implying that they talked directly with one another.

The Almighty continued to make His wishes known to His spokesmen throughout the Old Testament. Such encounters naturally evoked feelings of awe and submission as human beings listened to the voice of God.

Abraham, the Friend of God

Through inspiration, the writer James gave one of Jehovah's spokesmen a special distinction. In James 2:23 Abraham "was called the Friend of God." This particular verse follows a number of verses that deal with works of obedience (James 2:14-22). Abraham, the father of the faithful, believed and trusted in God completely. Whatever God commanded, Abraham was willing to do, even though he must have been perplexed at times.

Imagine being told to leave family, friends and homeland to journey to a completely strange place, which God would give to him (Genesis 12:1-4; 13:14-17). Would we have had such faith?

Abraham was told that his descendants would inherit the land, even when He and Sarah had no children (Genesis 12:2). How would we have felt if we had waited 20 years for a promised son?

When Isaac was but a boy, God again spoke to Abraham and commanded His faithful servant to offer his son as a sacrifice (Genesis 22:1-19). The answer to all of God's promises lay on the stack of wood that day on Mount Moriah as Abraham raised his knife in obedience to God's commands. The friend of God had met the ultimate test of faith when the angel of the Lord called to him from heaven and halted the sacrifice. A ram, caught in the thicket by his horns, was offered in the place of Isaac. "Now I know that thou fearest God" (Genesis 22:12).

Abraham was indeed the friend of God. He had enough faith to obey God's commands, regardless of how senseless they must have appeared to be at the time. This friendship was based upon more than just a warm, loving relationship. Abraham had enough respect for God to be willing to obey His commands.

Friends of Christ

The same basis for friendship with the Lord is found in the pages of the New Testament. In John 15:14 Christ told His disciples, "Ye are my friends, if ye do whatsoever I command you." This verse is preceded by the words: "Greater love hath no man than this, that a man lay down his life for his friends." Christ considered His disciples to be His friends and was nearing the time when He would show the ultimate in love by sacrificing His life for them. In return, He had every right to expect His followers to demonstrate their love for Him by keeping His commandments. The bond of friendship between Christ and His disciples was far more than just a warm feeling. Their friendship was equipped with the wheels of action: the giving of a life and the obedience to commands.

In summarizing the friendships of Abraham with God and Christ with His disciples, we can say that these friendships were based upon obeying the divine commands. Today, each of us undoubtedly has an individual view of this divine relationship. However, the most important factor on our part must be our willingness to obey His commands. As humans, we can never be perfect. God understands. We ask for His forgiveness in repentance and then accept His grace. Is this too much to be expected in view of the great display of love shown by the Father and the Son?

Three Persons of the Godhead

The Godhead is composed of three divine beings: God the Father, God the Son, and God the Holy Spirit. The Scriptures state that all three were present at the Creation (Genesis 1:26) and also at the baptism of Jesus (Mark 1:10-11). Our friendship with God is made complete by the threefold nature of the Trinity.

God the Father. Jehovah evokes our adoration, awe and praise. "God sitteth upon the throne of his holiness" (Psalm 47:8). Revelation abounds with language of majesty as it depicts the Father, sitting upon a royal throne and receiving the adoration of all around Him.

As human beings we should never forget the awe and magnificence of Jehovah. In the model prayer that Christ gave to His disciples, both the beginning and the conclusion are adorned with words of praise (Matthew 6:9, 13). It is significant that we enter and leave His presence with praise on our lips and a sense of awe in our hearts.

God the Son. In Luke's account of the birth of Christ, the angel Gabriel announced to the virgin Mary: "And, behold, thou shalt conceive in thy womb, and bring forth a son, and shalt call his name Jesus. ... The Holy Ghost shall come upon thee, and the power of the Highest shall overshadow thee: therefore also that holy thing which shall be born of thee shall be called the Son of God" (Luke 1:31, 35).

Matthew's account states, "That which is conceived in her is of the Holy Ghost" (Matthew 1:20).

Through the efforts of all three members of the Godhead, Christ left the splendors of heaven to be born in a stable. As a young boy, He undoubtedly walked the streets of Nazareth and played on the hillsides of Galilee. Early in life He learned the trade of being a carpenter, and His calloused hands undoubtedly knew the value of hard work. He ate with His friends (John 12:1-2). He cried with them (John 11:35). For 33 years the Son of God lived in a human body, experiencing the emotions that are common to mankind. Suspended on the cross between heaven and earth, Jesus shed His blood in the ultimate sacrifice for all of mankind. Today He sits on the right hand of God (Matthew 26:64), making intercession for the saints (Romans 8:34). As we ask God for help with our problems, Christ intercedes for us because He knows how we feel (Hebrews 4:15). In effect, He can say, "Father, I can sympathize for I, too, have been rejected and have known sorrow." (Also note Romans 8:34 and Hebrews 7:25.)

Most of us readily identify with this member of the Godhead as our friend. His contemporaries looked into His eyes as they talked with Him, felt His gaze (Luke 22:61), touched His hand (Luke 24:39), and undoubtedly shared moments of both happiness and sorrow. Vicariously, we can do the same. Thinking of Christ as our friend is much easier than calling Jehovah our daily companion. Yet, Christ said that it was through Him that the disciples could know His Father (John 14:7-11).

Christ lived in a human body, and He paid the price for His bride, the church (Ephesians 5:23; Revelation 21:9), with His own blood (Acts 20:28). The Son of God ascended to heaven, but He left His precious bride on this Earth. As Christians, we constitute that bride, the church. Our deep friendships naturally gravitate toward the members of that body, and within it we find our greatest earthly fulfillment in relationships.

God the Holy Spirit. Most Christians can readily identify with Christ as their daily companion and even can understand their relationships with the Father as one of profound respect and praise. Many of us, however, have more difficulty in conceiving of a relationship with the Holy Spirit. This third member of the Godhead is associated with miraculous manifestations throughout the Scriptures. On the Day of Pentecost, the Holy Spirit descended upon the apostles, enabling them to speak in unknown tongues, or languages other than their native tongues, as they taught the assembled (Acts 2:2-21). Through the mighty signs and wonders of the Holy Spirit, the words of the apostles were confirmed as being divine throughout their earthly ministries.

How can we, as mere humans, possibly conceive of a friendship with the Holy Spirit, who is so majestic and awe-inspiring?

True, most of us cannot imagine such a relationship. The Holy Spirit, however, has been responsible for placing something very tangible into our hands: the Scriptures. Also, the Comforter, or Holy Spirit, would enable the apostles to remember what Christ had taught them. They, in turn, would teach other people and write the divine message in the form of the Scriptures (John 14:26; 1 Timothy 3:16; John 16:13).

We may have difficulty fathoming a friendship with the Holy Spirit, but what faithful Christian cannot easily identify with the Bible? Its well-worn pages and underlined, favorite verses constitute a great gift from the Comforter. We may have trouble identifying with the Holy Spirit, but His tangible gift in our hands is a constant reminder of His love and concern.

Our Relationship with the Godhead. The members of the Godhead constitute a wonderful blending of friendship for us as mere human beings.

God the Father is majestic and awe-inspiring. We should never forget His magnificence nor our unworthiness when coming into

His presence. On the other hand, neither should we become negligent in remembering His great love for us in sending His Son (John 3:16). Christ, as He walked the paths of Palestine, was a combination of the human as well as the divine. We can identify with Him more easily. Through His bride, the church, we experience the divine institution composed of human beings. Whereas Christ left His bride with us, the Holy Spirit also gave us something tangible — the inspired Word of God. What wonderful friends we have with the awe-inspiring Godhead, and what tangible comforts we have been given in the form of the church and the Bible!

Contrasting Traits as Shown in Songs and Scriptures

The Almighty's personality has different facets. He is the inspiring God to be worshiped, and He is our daily companion. The Scriptures and the songs we sing reflect these concepts.

Songs. Thumb through your favorite song book and note the words. These are only a few of the songs that depict the majesty of God: "Christ, We Do All Adore Thee," "Come Thou Almighty King," "Praise God from Whom All Blessings Flow," "Hallelujah, Praise Jehovah," "Holy, Holy, Holy," "I Stand Amazed," "O Worship the King," "The Lord Is in His Holy Temple," "O Lord, Our Lord, How Excellent Is Thy Name," and "How Great Thou Art."

On the other hand, many of our hymns give expression to our friendship and companionship with God. Consider the words to these songs: "On and On We Walk Together," "I Traveled Down a Lonely Road," "I Come to the Garden Alone," "Does Jesus Care," "Closer to Thee," "Hold to God's Unchanging Hand," "No One Ever Cared for Me Like Jesus," "What a Friend We Have in Jesus," "God Shall Wipe Away All Tears," "Hand in Hand with Jesus," "I'll Be a Friend to Jesus," "Jesus, Hold My Hand," "Do You Know My Jesus?" and "My God and I."

Scriptures. The Bible abounds with verses that depict the majesty of God as well as our friendship with Him. For example, a perusal of the book of Psalms unfolds several viewpoints of the manner in which we conceive of God.

The epitome of our closeness to God is captured in the words of Psalm 23. Within these verses may be found a description of a most loving, tender and trusting relationship.

A sense of praise and majesty may be found in these Psalms:

"I ... will sing praise to the name of the Lord most high" (7:17).

"O Lord our Lord, how excellent is thy name in all the earth!" (8:1).

"I will praise thee, O Lord, with my whole heart" (9:1).

"The heavens declare the glory of God" (19:1).

"His praise shall continually be in my mouth" (34:1).

"For God is the King of all the earth: sing ye praises with understanding" (47:7).

"Sing forth the honor of his name: make his praise glorious" (66:2).

Other verses in Psalms describe still another facet of God's character. He also can condemn unrepenting sinners to everlasting punishment. Note these expressions:

"O Lord, rebuke me not in thine anger, neither chasten me in thy hot displeasure" (6:1).

"There is no soundness in my flesh because of thine anger" (38:3).

"O God, why hast thou cast us off for ever? why doth thine anger smoke against the sheep of thy pasture?" (74:1).

"How long, Lord? wilt thou hide thyself for ever? shall thy wrath burn like fire?" (89:46).

Still other verses voice the writers' view of God as one who can grant our petitions:

"Preserve me, O God: for in thee do I put my trust" (16:1).

"The Lord is my rock, and my fortress, and my deliverer" (18:2).

"Hear, O Lord, when I cry with my voice" (27:7).

"Hear the voice of my supplications, when I cry unto thee" (28:2).

"For he hath delivered me out of all trouble" (54:7).

"O my God, make haste for my help" (71:12).

Our Relationship with God

What a wonderful relationship we have with God! While evoking our awe and wonder, He also offers the same warm, tender relationship that a shepherd experiences with His fragile lambs. Christ left something tangible with us — His church, filled with other Christians who are there for us in good times and bad. While the nature of God the Holy Spirit is difficult for us to comprehend, He has placed in our hands a constant companion — the Bible. What a blessing!

Thus, we can see that God has many different facets in His nature. The manner in which we view these various characteristics depends upon our circumstances at a particular stage of our lives. Sometimes we view Him as a close friend. At other times He is the awesome king. Sometimes He is primarily seen as the one who can grant our petitions. Other moments may call to our realization His ability to punish people who are rebellious to His wishes. If the writers of the Psalms could understand the many-faceted nature of God, why can't we also comprehend His varied characteristics? He is all of these things to us.

Talking to God

We all want companions who are loving and caring. We seek people who will be loyal and steadfast, no matter what the circumstances of life might be. We expect friends to listen and understand our frustrations. We also yearn to be able to relax and be ourselves. We want forgiveness when we have erred and an acceptance of our frailties as humans. Because God has all these traits, and many more, what a wonderful friend He is!

First Thessalonians 5:17 admonishes Christians to pray without ceasing. Talking to God should be meshed with every aspect of our daily living as we go about our regular routines and as we set aside longer periods of time for talking with the Father. Daniel certainly had a regular habit of prayer. When the decree forbidding prayer was issued by King Darius, Daniel prayed "as he did aforetime" (Daniel 6:10).

Jesus, after urging His followers not to make a show of their prayers, gave them a model prayer with seven different parts (Matthew 6:9-13):

1. Praise: "Our Father which art in heaven, Hallowed be thy name." Too many times we forget to praise God in prayer. Because we are mere human beings, it is good to realize the majesty of the Father into whose presence we are entering. Christians should search the Scriptures for phrases of praise to God and make note of them to be used in daily prayers.

2. Church: "Thy kingdom come." Because the church had not yet been established at the time Christ gave the model prayer, the disciples were urged to pray for her coming. (See Matthew 3:2; 16:18-19; Luke 9:27; 22:29-30; John 3:3-5; Colossians 1:13). On the Day of Pentecost, the church was established, and we no longer word our prayers in this manner. However, this would be a good time to thank God for the bride of Christ and also to pray for her work and her leaders. We should be specific and mention certain needs and programs and the names of the elders and deacons. This part of our prayer could include our petitions for fellow Christians who are wayward and for brothers and sisters who are facing particular difficulties. It is also a good time to pray for people we have been teaching and trying to lead to Jesus.

3. Submission to God's Will: "Thy will be done in earth, as it is in heaven." Sometimes human beings have difficulty submitting their wills totally to the Father, but we can be of little real value to Him unless our lives become the vessels for doing His will on this earth. How many times do we approach God in prayer with a long list of our requests instead of opening our lives as channels for the furtherance of His plans? Our requests should be as specific as the man who requested three loaves of bread for his guest (Luke 11:5-10). If our petitions are not specific, how will we know whether or not they have been granted? We make our wishes known and then offer our lives in submission to His will, regardless of whether or not we approve of God's answers.

4. Requests for Essentials: "Give us this day our daily bread." Note that the disciples were never instructed to pray for enough food to last through the end of the month or until the next year. They were to ask for daily essentials.

This part of our prayer would present an excellent opportunity for thanking God for giving us all the essentials of life and for so many extras. Be specific. Thank Him for the new outfit you are wearing and the new curtains that make your home more enjoyable.

5. Forgiveness: "And forgive us our debts, as we forgive our debtors." We Christians can never expect to be forgiven of sin until we confess our own wrongs and, in turn, forgive people who have wronged us. This part of our prayer is the time to be specific about the wrongs that we have committed both in deeds and in attitudes. This time in our prayers will bring about a forgiving heart toward people who have wronged us. Remember that we cannot be forgiven ourselves until we first forgive people who have wronged us.

6. Help for Our Weaknesses: "And lead us not into temptation, but deliver us from evil." Each of us is vulnerable to the wiles of Satan. We all need to stop and mention our weaknesses specifically while we ask God's help in overcoming them.

7. Praise: "For thine is the kingdom, and the power, and the glory, for ever." Note that the model prayer begins and ends with praise for God. How often do we omit this part?

In addition to these parts of the model prayer, we, as Christians, would want to pray about many other areas: family members in need of help, sick friends, people with special problems, and many other people. Certainly, nothing is wrong with keeping a list of special requests to help us remember, provided the list is not conducive to making our prayers mechanical.

Because Christ is our intercessor, all prayers should acknowledge our privilege of having Him take our requests before the Father (Hebrews 7:25). We always pray in the name of Christ.

Some people keep a prayer journal. Instead of offering only oral prayers that sometimes wander, some find it helpful to write their prayers in a journal. This method helps keep one's mind on the subject and is an excellent means of refreshing memories as one looks back to previous months and realizes what God's answers have been.

Life is lived today in the fast lane. Our feet hit the ground running in the morning, and seldom do they slow down all day long. Little time is set aside to begin the day with a long prayer, and most of us are sound asleep by the time our heads hit the pillow. God never told us that our prayers must all be prayed at one particular time of the day. Nothing would be wrong with breaking the parts of the model prayer into smaller segments and praying the different sections throughout the day.

For example, have a prayer of praise for all the wonderful things our majestic Father has given to us as you shower early in the morning. Pray for the church during the time of dressing and applying makeup. Petition for people with special needs on the way to work. Ask for forgiveness throughout the day; we dare not wait until bedtime. On and on the list goes. In other words, incorporate all phases of your prayers into your life and truly pray without ceasing. Try changing posture during prayer; it is amazing how much easier it is to keep one's mind on praying when on bended knee.

Remember, God always answers the prayers of His children. Sometimes the answer is yes. At other times the reply is a simple no. Still other prayers elicit the response: "It is not best at this time." If we do not occasionally look over our prayer requests, how can we realize what the answers must have been?

God Talks to Us

Years ago Nathaniel Hawthorne penned a classic short story called "The Great Stone Face." A certain town was graced by a stone cliff that bore the resemblance of a man. The folklore of the townspeople prophesied the arrival of a man whose countenance would look like that of the Great Stone Face. Ernest, a young boy of the town, grew up in these surroundings and anxiously awaited the fulfillment of this promise. Eminent men came to the town, including a merchant, a soldier, a statesman and a poet. The local people hoped each would bear a resemblance to the Great Stone Face. One by one their hopes were aborted. Ernest, who had become the sage of the town when he grew to maturity, also felt disappointment about the lack of fulfillment of this prophecy as he gazed day after day at the stone visage on the mountainside. One day a visitor to the community happened to notice that it was Ernest who bore the resemblance to the Great Stone Face. Years of gazing lovingly at the image on the mountainside had transformed Ernest's face into the same features.

Hawthorne's story is fictitious, but Paul told the Corinthians about a spiritual transformation that is quite real. In 2 Corinthians 3:18 the writer says, "But we all, with open face beholding as in a glass the glory of the Lord, are changed into the same image from glory to glory, even as by the Spirit of the Lord."

Notice that an open face is necessary, a complete submission to God's will. Just as one might lovingly behold an image in a glass day after day until she gradually assumes the same appearance, even so is a Christian changed into the likeness of Christ by gazing upon His image. Looking upon the physical appearance of Christ is not intimated in the passage. Paul was permitted to witness the resurrected Christ to qualify him for the apostleship, but even this miraculous manifestation was not enough. Paul was told to enter the city of Damascus, where he would be told what he must do to be saved (Acts 9:6). We are told what we must do through His Word, and it is through this perfect law of liberty that we behold the image necessary to our transformation. As Christians, we lovingly read of the nature of Christ through the Word until we gradually become more and more like Him.

Good friends love to talk with one another. The relationship is not strained, and no awkward fumbling for words occurs. Sometimes good friends enjoy the beauty and richness of silence in one another's presence. The same is true of our friendship with God. Talking with Him in prayer throughout the day is as natural as breathing. Listening to Him talk to us through the Word also should be just as natural as praying.

Most of us want to spend more time in Bible study, but two culprits hinder our good intentions. First, we are all guilty, to some degree, of being too busy and too rushed. Second, most of us lack direction in our study. We aimlessly shift from one method of Bible study to another.

Paul admonished young Timothy to study to show himself approved unto God as he rightly divided the Word of Truth (2 Timothy 2:15). The people at Berea were more noble than the Thessalonians because they received the Word with readiness of mind and searched the Scriptures daily to determine whether these things were true (Acts 17:11).

Remembering that time in study of God's Word is time spent in listening to a friend may enhance your Bible Study. Perhaps the suggestions given here will help you:

• Select a comfortable place for study, and keep your materials within easy reach. Invest in good reference books. We usually purchase whatever is most important to us.

• Be realistic in your time allotments. It is not necessary to spend hours poring over the printed page. A realistic 15 minutes a day, faithfully kept, eventually will produce dramatic results. Select the time of day when your mind is at its peak. Some brains function best in the early morning hours, while others do not become alert until the sun goes down. You will have to exert control over yourself until this daily appointment with God become automatic.

• Begin your quiet time with a prayer for an open mind to God's words. You probably also will want to pause to talk to your heavenly Father in the midst of a study.

• Choose a method of study:

1. A-chapter-a-day is one method of study used by many. Other people try to read through the entire Bible in a year.

2. Select one of the Gospels, and study a small portion each day. In a notebook, rewrite each verse in your own words. Draw maps to help you vicariously walk with Christ throughout His homeland. Using a harmony of the Gospels is also helpful.

3. Study one epistle. Choose one letter, and duplicate the book from a large-print edition. Paste one or two verses on a blank page in a loose-leaf notebook. Use your concordances, commentaries and other study guides to help you better understand the nuances of word meanings. Consult maps and other helps. Write your findings on the page where that verse has been pasted. Do not rush. One epistle may require several months of study, but think of the wealth of knowledge you will have acquired over a period of 20 or 30 years! In effect, you will have written your own commentaries on

those books. The notebooks will become some of your prized possessions.

4. Study by subjects. Select a topic such as worship, baptism, church organization, etc. Use your concordance or topical Bible to help you locate all the verses on a given subject. Write them in a notebook that is a convenient size to carry with you. You will find that you have developed a valuable aid for studying with someone whenever these subjects arise and you have an opportunity to teach.

5. Choose a Bible-related subject such as evolution. Read articles, and know what is being taught. Then search the Scriptures to find answers. Keep the articles and your Bible research in file folders. This wealth of information will be precious in the years to come.

6. Study the geography of Palestine. Learning about Bible lands deepens your understanding of the Bible. Good workbooks and even videos about this subject are available. A general basic course is profitable for building a foundation.

7. Invest in workbooks on different subjects. A Christian does not have to be in a class to make good use of workbooks. Mark your answers as you study.

8. Read surveys of the different books of the Bible. Sometimes we can become bogged down in our studies. Although reading a few verses at a time and learning all shades of meaning is an excellent means of studying, sometimes we cannot see the forest for the trees.

9. Make a special study of favorite Bible characters. Learn all you can about the lives of these people and the lessons that are applicable today. Keep your notes.

10. Subscribe to several periodicals. Read widely from a representative sample of brotherhood publications and be knowledgeable of current trends and movements. Compare the writings to the Word of God.

• Study with a friend. Most of your studying will be done alone, but it is good to get together with a friend to exchange ideas on your respective studies. For a husband and wife to study together on a daily basis is wonderful.

• Listen to tapes of the Scriptures. So many household tasks are performed routinely. Although the hands are busy, the mind is free. Listen to the reading of whole books of the Bible as you take a bath, put on makeup, exercise, clean kitchen cabinets, or do other routine things. An epistle can become much more meaningful when you listen to the words being read aloud in one sitting as they were long ago. Also, profit from tapes of sermons and class studies.

• Place verses of Scripture in conspicuous areas. Use your kitchen sink, bathroom mirror, desk at work, dash of your car, and other prominent places to take advantage of spare minutes while you are busy doing routine tasks. Verses are memorized effortlessly and quickly by this method.

• Use spare minutes wisely. How many times have we wasted at least an hour at a doctor's office by thumbing through magazines that are several years old? Instead, before you leave the house for any event that might involve waiting for even a few minutes, take along some of your study material. The years roll by, and those small pockets of minutes can provide time for acquiring vast amounts of knowledge and understanding.

God's Word is indeed a treasure that should be laid in our hearts as He talks with us.

An ancient fable tells about three merchants who were crossing the Arabian Desert, traveling at night to escape the heat. While crossing a dry creek bed, a voice told them to stop and pick up pebbles from the creek bed and put them in their pockets. The merchants then were told to leave that area and camp for the remainder of the night. In the morning they would be both happy and sad. The next day they found jewels in their pockets. Indeed, they were happy because they had picked up the pebbles and put them in their pockets. Conversely, they also were sad because they had not picked up more while they had an opportunity. May we not come to the last years of our lives and regret that we did not gather more precious nuggets of gold from the Word of God.

My God and I

The words of the song "My God and I" have always been especially meaningful to me. Although God now communicates through the written Word and no longer speaks directly to His children as He once did with Abraham, Moses and many other Bible characters, the words of the song are still significant to us today. The mature Christian realizes that the language is figurative, but the sentiment expressed is one of extreme closeness and tenderness between God and His child. The song expresses this relationship by using the comparison of two friends walking and talking with clasped hands as they laugh together.

Do you feel close enough to God to share your joys with Him? Have you ever cried while figuratively leaning on His shoulder? Is He your daily companion in all that you do?

Friendships with human beings are empty and meaningless until we first take the time to cultivate our relationships with God. We talk to Him through prayer and He communicates to us through His Word.

"We walk and talk as good friends should and do."

Questions

1. Discuss the different concepts of God that were given in the introduction to this lesson, and add others in the class discussion. Why does God seem to mean so many different things to different people? Is this good or bad?
2. How did God talk with the patriarchs? What marred the relationship of God with Adam and Eve?
3. Read Exodus 3:6; 33:11, 20. Did Moses ever see the face of Jehovah?
4. Abraham was given the distinction of being called the friend of God in James 2:23. He also probably is known best for his faithfulness to the Father. In what ways did Abraham show his faithfulness? What is the connection between being a friend of God and obeying His commands?
5. Upon what condition were the disciples the friends of Christ (John 15:14)? What is the similarity in Abraham's being called

the friend of God and in the disciples' being called friends of
Jesus? What is the lesson for us today? Does this in any way
dispel a feeling of closeness?

6. What are the distinctive characteristics of each member of
the Godhead? Is there a difference in the way we feel about
each one?

7. God the Father gave mankind a very tangible gift in the form of
His Son, who inhabited a human body for 33 years. What tangible gift did Christ leave for the world? What tangible gift
did the Holy Spirit give to us? Discuss the importance of these
tangible gifts to human beings.

8. Sing together the first lines of several songs that depict the
majesty of God. Sing others that express our closeness and
friendship with Him. Why do you think there is a contrast in
our singing?

9. From Psalms, discuss verses that show different facets in God's
nature. The lesson mentioned four characteristics; can you find
more? Is there any discrepancy in these divergent viewpoints?
How do you personally regard God?

10. What are some qualities we generally look for in our friends?
How many of these does God possess?

11. We talk to God through the avenue of prayer. What does it mean
to pray without ceasing (1 Thessalonians 5:17)?

12. What are the seven main parts of the model prayer in Matthew
6:9-13? Divide the class into even parts for a discussion of each
of these divisions with a modern application of each.

13. How can you find more time to devote to prayer? Use the suggestions mentioned in the lesson in addition to your own.

14. What are God's three primary responses to our prayers? Why
do we often feel that our prayers have not been answered if
the answer seems to be no?

15. Why is it important for us to improve our Bible study? Discuss
the suggestions for Bible study and add your own ideas.

16. How can being too busy or lacking direction in our Bible study
prevent our listening to God?

17. Why is a proper relationship with God necessary before we can develop friendships with other people?
18. When have you felt closest to God? Can our relationship with Him be based entirely upon feelings? Why?
19. Have you ever reached out for God and felt that no one was there? Who moved?
20. According to Ephesians 3:17, how does Christ dwell in us? How do we obtain that faith (Romans 10:17)? What is the application for us today?

Our Friendship with Ourselves

The yearning to have friends is a basic human instinct. Many people read books and strive to learn better relationship techniques. Somehow they think that if they practice certain social skills, people will be drawn to them magnetically. Such Band-Aid measures, however, are only superficial. All too often the problem lies within. They never have mastered the art of being friends with themselves; consequently, they cannot extend the hand of friendship. If people do not like themselves, they certainly cannot like others.

"Though we travel the world over to find the beautiful, we must carry it with us or we find it not." — Ralph Waldo Emerson

Biblical Foundation

We are commanded to love ourselves. Matthew 22:34-40 relates the incident of a lawyer's trying to trap Christ with the question,

"Master, which is the great commandment in the law?" The Son of God replied, "Thou shalt love the Lord thy God with all thy heart, and with all thy soul, and with all thy mind. This is the first and great commandment. And the second is like unto it, Thou shalt love thy neighbor as thyself."

Loving God must be paramount in our lives. We have little trouble in accepting this as the greatest commandment, but sometimes we tend to reverse the remaining two when we place loving other people before loving ourselves. If we do not love ourselves, we cannot love other people. If we cannot feel comfortable with ourselves, then it is impossible to be at ease with other people.

Loving ourselves has nothing to do with conceit, arrogance, or an infatuated sense of self-worth. People who display such negative characteristics do not have a very high regard for themselves. Trying to impress people by such measures is a defensive mechanism that is designed to inflate one's own ego. If we are truly our own friends and accept ourselves, there is no need to try to parade our superior qualities before the world. Other people eventually will discover whatever we have to offer.

As has been stated wisely, we do not love ourselves for who we are but because of whose we are.

In the very beginning God said,

> "Let us make man in our image, after our likeness. ... So God created man in his own image, in the image of God created he him; male and female created he them. ... And God saw every thing that he had made, and, behold, it was very good" (Genesis 1:26-27, 31).

Sin started in the Garden and has continued through the ages. Mankind has done many terrible things, and yet the Father loves us so much that He gave His only Son in a horrible death in order that we might have eternal life (John 3:16). A great price was paid for our redemption: "the precious blood of Christ, as of a lamb without blemish and without spot" (1 Peter 1:19). "But God commendeth his love toward us, in that, while we were yet sinners, Christ died for us" (Romans 5:8).

Indeed, we were bought with a great price, and we remain special in God's sight. The New Testament epistles are filled with words of rebuke and correction for the wrongs committed by the first-century Christians, but God still loved each one. Over and over He begged His children to repent because He cared for them.

The realization that we are very special to God should be the foundation for friendship with ourselves.

A Contrast

We tend to wear different masks to conceal our real feelings, not only from other people but also from ourselves. The surface may seem smooth; yet, how often do we experience inner turmoil? Sometimes we are the last ones to see ourselves as we really are under all the layers of protective coverings that we build around ourselves. Each must make friends with this inner person, the true self.

Many traits usually characterize a person who does not love herself and is, consequently, not her own friend. She often feels troubled, discouraged, depressed, helpless, anxious, inferior, isolated and unloved. She is frequently oversensitive about her feelings and has poor friend relationships.

In an effort to conceal these deep feelings, one who does not love herself may resort to such defensive measures as bragging and arrogance to make people think she is important.

By way of contrast, a person who has made friends with herself has no need to impress anyone else with her own worth. She certainly is aware of her limitations and weaknesses, but she uses them as springboards for improvement. She feels confident and useful and is well adjusted, not because of her attainments but rather because of her value in God's sight.

A Valuable Airborne Lesson

As the flight attendant began her message, I started to block out the instructions, which I had heard countless times before. On this particular trip, however, some of her words caught my attention: "In the event of an emergency, adults who are traveling with a small child should first place their own oxygen masks in the correct position before attempting to assist those who are young and in need of assistance."

The familiar words suddenly took on new meaning as I realized their full impact. At first the thought of snatching an oxygen mask and putting it on myself before caring for a small child seemed so selfish. After pondering for a few moments, however, the reason was apparent. If I could not function properly, I would be of little use in assisting a helpless one to safety.

Before I can even consider being a friend to anyone else by sharing her joys and sorrow, I first must be able to stand on my own two feet. I have to be my own person, my own best friend, before I can offer the hand of friendship to people around me. If I do not take care of myself, I can do little for anyone else.

Guidelines for Dealing with Friends

In an initial study about friendship, I asked the participants how they tried to treat their best friends. A brainstorming session revealed these qualities: acceptance, respect, love, a listening ear, gentleness, concern for their well being, patience, honesty, courtesy, intuitively tuning in to their needs, encouragement in reaching their full potential, faithfulness, open-mindedness, seeking their best interest, forgiving.

How sad it is that we frequently treat others better than we treat ourselves! So often we criticize and put ourselves down until there is little left but a skeleton of our full potential.

In a nutshell, we might say that we should show ourselves the same respect and consideration that we extend to our best friends.

Becoming Better Friends with Ourselves

Luke 2:52 notes, "And Jesus increased in wisdom and stature, and in favor with God and man." The Son of God matured in all phases of His life as He developed intellectually, physically, spiritually and socially.

Like Christ, we humans have different facets in our makeup. If we are going to be friends with ourselves, we should strive to develop fully in all areas: our intellect, our physical and emotional beings, and our spiritual relationship with God, as well as our relationships with other people.

We must be willing to examine our lives and assume the responsibility for the way we live. Plato wisely observed that the life that is unexamined is not worth living. A vast difference exists between being alone and being lonely. Christ withdrew from the demanding crowds for periods of solitude. Introspection requires time to be alone and ask honest questions. Solitude is a time to learn to be friends with ourselves.

How sad it is to go through life with false assumptions that could have been corrected, guilt that could have been lifted, or undesirable traits that could have been lessened if only we had bothered to take charge of our lives and had ventured to look beneath the protective coverings that camouflage the real person.

Just as we want what is best for any of our true friends, so should we desire the same for ourselves. We must take the time to set realistic goals for whatever is required to aid us in reaching our full potential in all phases of our lives: the spiritual, physical, emotional, intellectual and social parts of our nature. These goals should help us stretch and grow without being so idealistic that they are impossible, thus causing a very frustrated and unhappy existence.

"Whether you think you can or you can't, you are probably right." — Henry Ford

Physical

How often do we neglect our physical bodies, treating them with neglect and utter lack of regard for their well-being? In an effort to climb the ladder of success, we frequently sacrifice our health. A misused body finds it difficult to concentrate on the more abstract phases of life. Thinking about spiritual matters when we are exhausted is difficult. A sick body has trouble sorting through faulty emotions in an effort to replace them with constructive thoughts. A person who has been overcome with stress is not likely to take the necessary time to interact with people and develop friendships. A failure to care for our physical bodies is tantamount to killing the goose that lays the golden eggs.

Our Physical Health. Paul reminded the Christians at Corinth, "Know ye not that your body is the temple of the Holy Ghost which is in you, which ye have of God, and ye are not your own? For ye are bought with a price: therefore glorify God in your body, and in your spirit, which are God's" (1 Corinthians 6:19-20).

After the confrontation with the prophets of Baal on Mount Carmel, Elijah fled from the wrath of Jezebel to the wilderness of Beersheba, where he sat under a juniper tree to await death. Utter emotional and physical exhaustion prompted the deep sleep that his body needed. An angel touched the prophet and greeted him with the welcome news that water and bread were waiting. Elijah's physical body had to be cared for properly before he could continue on God's spiritual mission (1 Kings 19:4-8).

We are all busy and constantly on the run, eating improperly and failing to get adequate rest. If we do not fuel our bodies with the right nourishment, and if we deprive them of needed rest, they will not function efficiently. Just as important as food and rest are exercise and proper medical treatment. Remember, if we do not take care of the goose, there will be no golden eggs.

Our Physical Appearance. If we listen to commercials, most of us would be convinced that the way to a happy life is based solely upon the right kind of cosmetics, a trim body, and the latest in fashions. If friendship with ourselves is founded solely upon our physical appearance, we are in for big trouble! Despite all moisturizers, some wrinkles eventually will appear. Bodies inevitably have a tendency to shift the weight and thicken in the middle. Financial reversals could limit our supply of fashionable clothes.

Although we cannot base our friendship with ourselves upon our appearance, taking care of the physical appearance does play a part in our outlook on life. All too well, I personally know the shock of awakening one day to an altered face after my original one had been crushed in an automobile accident. Seventeen years passed before I could fully accept the new face. The emotional blows were cushioned by the realization that I am God's child and am very special to Him. A loving husband eased the emotional pain by making me feel that I was beautiful in his eyes and by buying many new outfits to help me feel more attractive. At that particular time in my life, concentrating upon improving the physical appearance was a factor in my recovery.

By way of summary, we could say that we are being friends to ourselves when we properly care for our physical bodies and also make them look as attractive as possible without basing our self-concept upon the way we look.

Intellectual

Realizing that any part of our bodies will atrophy if not properly used and stimulated, we should challenge our minds continually to learn new facts and skills:

1. Upon completion of formal schooling, many people often see little need for further education and their minds slowly die. The stimulation of learning new things is invigorating to the mind. The urgent demands of everyday living usually crowd out our growth in intellectual areas unless we have previously set goals to continue our learning.

2. Select a subject or a skill, and set out to master it. A mind that is challenged constantly increases in its ability to conquer new fields.

3. Bible study not only expands the mind, but it also feeds the soul.

Emotional

Sometimes we find it easier to accept the fact that our physical bodies require care than to realize that our emotions must also receive proper maintenance.

If we are true friends to ourselves, we will examine the thoughts that constantly run through our minds in an effort to determine whether they are building us up or tearing us down. "For as he thinketh in his heart, so is he" (Proverbs 23:7). "Keep thy heart with all diligence; for out of it are the issues of life" (Proverbs 4:23).

1. It is just as important to provide rest for our emotions as it is to give our bodies a chance to sleep. We all need regular relaxation and diversions. But people respond differently. What is relaxing to one may produce great strain and stress for another. Whatever hobby or diversion enables us to break the circuit and provide a period of restoration to our emotions is a wise investment of the time involved. Ideally, our life's work and recreation should revolve around those activities that satisfy and bring pleasure.

2. So many demands are placed upon our time. How often does the urgent require our every waking moment and the important is crowded out completely? Errands always need to be run. Jobs consume hours each day. Meals must be cooked. Clothes must be washed. Bills must be paid. On and on the list could go. Frequently, we get to the end of the day or week and realize that some very important things in our lives have been neglected. Little Johnny had clean clothes, cooked meals, and was transported to ball games; but no time was found to talk with him about important values in his life. Our husbands had all the physical necessities provided for them, but there was no time to linger over a cup of coffee after dinner and just talk. We were too exhausted at the end of the day to communicate with God through prayer and listen to Him through His Word. We will never solve this age-old problem until we get our priorities in order.

3. We must refuse to allow the past to dominate the present as well as the future. Early childhood experiences leave a deep impression upon the mind of a child. He reacts either positively or negatively to whatever is fed into the subconscious mind with little reasoning ability. If someone constantly is run down, criticized, shamed, insulted or seldom praised, then naturally he accepts this assessment as the truth. Children can be verbally cruel to one another, and the blows leave emotional scars. As we reach the maturity of adult years, we are being friends to ourselves when we sort through the maze of voices that shaped our childhood and rid ourselves of the damaging ones.

4. Our emotional lives will be healthier if we realize we do not have to excel in everything. It is wise to put certain terms in their proper perspectives:

  a. Self-image refers to the way we see ourselves. We may think we are painfully ugly although we are actually quite attractive in the eyes of others.

  b. Self-confidence is our belief in an ability to perform well in certain areas. For example, we may have absolutely no athletic skills, but we may possess superior knowledge in computer science. The inability to throw or catch a ball should not cause us to feel inadequate. We should be mature enough to realize that no person can do all things well. Instead of lamenting our deficiencies, we should focus on our strengths. When we zero in on our good points and develop them fully, we are better able to deal with our weaknesses.

 c. Mirrored image is the picture of ourselves as it is reflected from others by the tone of their voices, their glances and their touches. Fortunate is the person who received positive reflections as a child. If they were negative ones, we should have the maturity to tear down the walls we allowed others to build around our personalities and thus free ourselves to live more abundantly.

 d. Self-esteem is the way we feel about ourselves as contrasted with the way we see ourselves. We may have the knowledge that we are lacking in some area, which is normal. Yet, we can feel good about ourselves and be our own friend. This evaluation requires maturity.

 5. We should develop a thicker skin regarding harsh criticism. Realize that everyone who tries to do anything probably will be criticized by someone, and be aware of the fact that a critical person usually feels inferior and uses criticism as a defensive mechanism to build herself up. Examine the criticism for the inherent germ of truth, profit from it, and drop the shackles of the unkind remark.

 6. Realize that anger can be a healthy emotion. It acts as a red flag to the emotional system to alert it to the fact that something is wrong. How we react to anger determines whether it is good or bad.

 7. We must be able to stand on our own feet emotionally. We cannot manipulate other people just because we are lonely and need friends.

Social

 Other people are an important part of our lives. You, the reader, would probably not be engaging in this study unless you realized this truth.

 1. Accept the fact that we all need friends, whether one is shy or the life of the party. Some need friends more than others, but everyone's life is enriched through the blessing of special friendships.

2. Two views must be properly focused. First, we should look within and try to make our own lives what they should be. Our own attitudes affect the manner in which we see people. If we are suspicious, intolerant and overcritical of ourselves, we tend to believe that everyone else possesses these same traits. Sometimes we are our own worst enemy.

Second, if our perspective of people is faulty, we should try to seek the good in them. When we think of most people as basically good, we will be attracted to them.

3. We should try to cultivate a wide range of friendships, realizing that our closest friends will rise to the top. We would not be friends to ourselves if we tolerated life without the beauty of friendships.

Spiritual

We can be friends to ourselves physically, intellectually, emotionally, as well as socially, and yet all our efforts will be futile if we fail to nurture our spiritual beings because the soul lives forever. Even if we fall short in other areas, our lives will not be in vain if we are victorious spiritually.

1. We are special in God's sight. He loved each of us enough to give His own Son for our redemption (John 3:16).

2. God should be the Lord of our lives. As long as we alone try to control, we cannot succeed. Only when we submit our will to Him can we realize true spiritual victory. "I can do all things through Christ which strengtheneth me" (Philippians 4:13). God does not need our adoration. It is we who are uplifted through worship.

3. We must learn to forgive. All too often we go through life, weighted down with a bag of grievances. Someone makes a remark that irritates us. We stuff the memory of it into a grievance bag. Another slights us, and we take offense. Into the same bag goes this hurt. On and on the story continues until we eventually find ourselves staggering under the load. The sooner we can rid ourselves of such negative emotions, the happier we will be.

Having our feelings hurt is not the same as having someone sin against us. We should be mature enough to forget the slights. If someone actually has sinned against us, however, we have the obligation to go to him concerning the wrong lest he be lost eternally (Matthew 18:15; Luke 17:3-4). If we have sinned against anyone, then we are commanded to go to that person and immediately make the matter right (Matthew 5:23-24). The Christian has the responsibility of settling the grievance, regardless of who is at fault.

4. We must learn to accept forgiveness. So often we pick up books that urge us to love and accept ourselves unconditionally. However, at times we should feel despair. Just as the publican beat on his breast and asked God to "be merciful to me a sinner" (Luke 18:13), so should our consciences be pricked when we realize we have transgressed the law of God. After we have confessed our wrongs in repentance and have made matters right to the best of our ability, we should believe God concerning His promises of forgiveness and accept His grace. "Confess your faults one to another, and pray one for another, that ye may be healed" (James 5:16). "If we confess our sins, he is faithful and just to forgive us our sins, and to cleanse us from all unrighteousness" (1 John 1:9).

5. We should learn to distinguish the difference between sin and ordinary blunders. Sin is the transgression of God's law (1 John 3:4). It must be confessed and forgiven.

A vast difference exists between sin and human blunders. How often do we put our feet in our mouths by blurting out an inappropriate remark or by taking an unwise action? Such a misstep is not a sin but merely part of being a member of the human race. How much happier we would be if we simply could learn to laugh at ourselves. As the saying goes, "Happy is he who can laugh at himself, for he will never cease to be amused." Each such mistake teaches us that a better way can be found to handle matters. Considered in perspective, mistakes are the stepping stones to growth.

We are being friends to ourselves when we learn to confess sin and accept God's forgiveness while acknowledging our human shortcomings as we daily strive to become more like Christ. Each of us is a mixture of good and bad.

Conclusion

Second only to our friendship with God is our relationship with ourselves. We can never feel at ease around people until we first feel comfortable with ourselves. Hiding under masks, which we so often wear to shield the real person, is only superficial. Other people can tell. We are all repelled by hypocrisy and attracted by openness.

Christians are mere human beings who have been cleansed by the blood of Christ. As we daily confess our wrongs and accept His forgiveness, we realize that we could never be good enough or so perfect that we could earn salvation.

Only God can take the broken pieces of our lives and create in them something beautiful. The Scriptures attest to this marvel, from the broken pitchers of Gideon's army (Judges 7:19-22) to the shattered alabaster box that played a part in the glorifying of our Lord (Mark 14:3-9).

Life not only is about getting to a destination; life is about having a fulfilling journey. Becoming friends with ourselves helps to make that possible. How sad it is to reach the end only to discover that one has never really lived.

Years ago our daughter cross-stitched some words that have been framed and occupy a prominent place in our home because they have been very meaningful: "What we are is God's gift to us. What we become is our gift to God."

Questions

1. Why do most people yearn to have friends? Why do we so often neglect friendship with ourselves?
2. Discuss Matthew 22:34-40. What three loves are given? Why is the order of the last two so often reversed?
3. Sometimes we equate conceit, bragging and arrogance with self-love. Is this right?
4. Discuss the statement, "We do not love ourselves for who we are but because of whose we are."
5. Read John 3:16, 1 Peter 1:19 and Romans 5:8. Did mankind de-

serve such a precious gift? What is the very least we can offer God in return?

6. Why should the realization that we are special to God be the foundation for friendship with ourselves?

7. What are some traits that characterize people who are not friends with themselves? What are some identifying marks for people who have accepted themselves as friends?

8. What is the rationale behind the theory that we must first take care of ourselves before we can be of any help to other people? Do you agree or disagree?

9. As a class, make a list of the ways in which you treat your friends. How many of these traits have you displayed toward yourself?

10. According to Luke 2:52, in what ways did Christ mature? How can these areas be a foundation for our relationship with ourselves?

11. Why is it necessary to stop, withdraw for a time, and examine our lives?

12. Goals help us stretch to our full potential. What is the danger of setting goals that are too idealistic?

13. Why is the health of our bodies important in serving God? Note 1 Corinthians 6:19-20 and 1 Kings 19:4-8. What can we do to better care for our physical bodies?

14. Can we place too much importance on our physical appearance? Does the way we look have a bearing on our outlook on life?

15. How can the intellectual part of our beings be strengthened?

16. Discuss seven ways we can promote better emotional health.

17. Name at least three considerations to be used in improving the social aspect of your life.

18. Why is the spiritual side of our beings more important than all the others? Discuss these considerations:

    a. We are special in God's sight.

    b. God should be the Lord of our lives.

    c. We must learn to forgive.

    d. We must learn to accept forgiveness.

    e. We should be able to distinguish the difference between sin and ordinary blunders.

19. Discuss the concept behind these words: "What we are is God's gift to us. What we become is our gift to God."
20. Divide the class into pairs, and ask each member of the couple to list the good qualities about the other person. Then have each couple share these lists with one another.

CHAPTER 4

HANDLE WITH CARE

The Seeds of Friendship, Pt. 1

Seeking the friendship of other people in order to lessen our own loneliness borders on selfishness. Although it is true that friendships are one of the greatest blessings of life, they are not to be sought actively. Rather, they form naturally as we trust God enough to follow His divine principles. Until our friendship with God is as it should be and until our friendship with ourselves is on solid ground, we always will have trouble relating to other people. The most important building block of any relationship is what we are. All too often we try to use the remedies of quick fixes to lessen the pain of loneliness, but we are only treating the symptoms instead of dealing with the problem.

Instead of seeking the companionship of other people, we should simply take God at His word and go through life scattering the seeds of friendship wherever we are. When those seeds fall into the fertile ground of receptive hearts, the flowers of friendship will develop.

Each flower of friendship is uniquely different, and no two are alike. Some will be roses; some will be lilies; others will be daffodils, violets or pansies. Some relationships offer companionship, some provide compassion, and others act as a refuge in times of trouble. The rainbow of differences enhances the beauty of the landscape of life.

Some seeds may sprout quickly and soon fade away. Other seeds may endure throughout a lifetime. But they are all important, and the garden of life indeed would be bleak without them.

Whatever is planted will bring its own fruit. "Be not deceived; God is not mocked: for whatsoever a man soweth, that shall he also reap" (Galatians 6:7). "But this I say, He which soweth sparingly shall reap also sparingly; and he which soweth bountifully shall reap also bountifully" (2 Corinthians 9:6).

Seed #1: Develop a Proper Perspective of Other People

Once a teacher appeared before her class with a shoe box that had holes in one end of the lid. After calling for two volunteers, she gave each of them a piece of paper that told what was in the box. Then she asked if they would like to insert a hand into the box and claim the contents. One person grew pale and shied away. The other one eagerly thrust her hand through the opening to receive the prize: a piece of chocolate candy.

What was the difference? On one slip of paper were the words "a piece of candy." The other paper bore the message, "a dead mouse." Regardless of the facts, few people will ever willingly expose themselves to anything they believe could cause displeasure if they have a choice in the matter.

In the same way, we react to other people according to our perception of them. If we perceive of most people as human beings who make mistakes, just as we do, but who need us and are basically good, receptive, warm and loving, then we will gravitate toward them. On the other hand, if we envision mankind as cruel, biting, and out to do us harm, then we will stand back just as did the girl who held the words "a dead mouse." It does not matter what the facts are. If we perceive of people as being hurtful, we are going to withdraw from them. The receptive person realizes that some friendships will go sour, but she is willing to take the risk in order to develop the good ones. After all, Babe Ruth struck out 1,330 times, but he also hit 714 home runs, which was a record for 40 years. He never would have had so many successes if he had been unwilling to try and risk the failures.

Our general perception of people influences our attitudes; our attitudes, in turn, determine our actions. Those actions are what other people see, and those actions greatly influence the way people respond to us. A cycle soon is formed. The people who believe other people are usually good and pleasurable generally attract a host of friends, which, in turn, motivates them to continue those attractive actions and draw even more friends. Such a person may not be the life of the party. In fact, she may be a little shy, but she genuinely loves people and seems to have a wealth of friends.

On the other hand, those people who are suspicious of the motives of everyone and who generally see people as causing pain naturally will withdraw into their shells. Such actions make other people even less responsive to them.

A person who sincerely loves other people will find that she is living in a loving world. The angry, suspicious person soon will discover that she lives in a hurtful world.

"The world is a looking glass and gives back to every man the reflection of his own face." — William Thackery

Seed #2: Make People a Priority

When we view people in general as pleasurable, making them a priority in our lives will be natural. We count our friends among our greatest blessings and are as proud of them as we would be of precious stones set in a necklace of gold.

So much of life is lived in the fast lane. We are so busy scurrying around to take care of the urgent that, all too often, we have no time for what is really important in life. Our mobile society, with its frequent moves, leaves little time for lasting relationships. Gone are the days of front porches, where neighbors gathered to talk during the evening hours while their children played in the yard. All too often we get to the end and realize that the lucrative careers, the fine homes, the newest cars and expensive clothes seem very empty if we have failed to make people a priority. Making friends does require time, and deep friendships require time for long talks. Friendships must be nurtured throughout our lives. We usually find time to do what we want to do. If people are important to us, we will find the necessary time to invest in them. Those who seem to do it effortlessly have usually developed skills they began to form early in life.

The rituals of friendship vary. Some people lunch together on a regular basis. Other friends take the time to remember long-distance birthdays with a card, a note of current news, and pictures of the family. I know of two families who have missed spending only two New Year's days together in the past 30 years. Keeping that day open for their get-togethers has been a priority for each family.

Too many of us are task-oriented rather than people-oriented. Getting a job done can be more important than taking the time to talk with a friend. People must be so valuable to us that we make them a priority in our own lives.

Seed #3: Circulate Among People

We all need friends, and the potential for blessings arising from friendships is limitless. However, those meaningful relationships will never develop as long as we isolate ourselves in our homes or in the work places and seldom mingle with others.

Many are lonely but won't admit it. Often it becomes easier to wear masks of complacency and indifference than to face the problem and take corrective measures. The chronic pain of loneliness sometimes becomes dulled by years of denial.

Sometimes effort is required to climb over our self-imposed walls and truly circulate among people in a meaningful way. As has been said, the journey of a thousand miles begins with one step. That first step may mean joining a club, participating in sports, doing volunteer work, pursuing a hobby, inviting others into one's home, baking cookies for a neighbor, or even sitting in a different section of the church building.

All too often we are surrounded by people, but our protective walls will not allow us truly to interact with them. Many potentially rich friendships never develop because of our own isolation. We must be willing to create an environment in which possible relationships can sprout, grow and flourish.

Seed #4: Take the Initiative in Reaching Out

Some very simple, but powerful, words are found in Proverbs 18:24: "A man that hath friends must show himself friendly."

Most of us probably never will know how many potential friendships have been lost simply because we did not exert the extra effort to offer friendliness whenever we have encountered strangers. A simple, but wise, bit of advice was written centuries ago: "Therefore all things whatsoever ye would that men should do to you, do ye even so to them" (Matthew 7:12).

Think about the different people who have floated in and out of your life through the years. Which ones captured your attention from the first moment you met? What was it about those people that triggered your desire to get to know them better?

Some seem to be born with skills for reaching out to people. Others want to be friendly but have not learned how to take advantage of the opportunities found in first contacts. The following simple, but often ignored, suggestions may be of help:

1. Realize the first impression is important. We never again have the chance to make a first impression upon that particular person.

2. Be the first to speak. Don't wait for others to take the initiative.

3. Smile. Frowning requires 72 muscles. Only 15 are needed for smiling. We are all attracted to a smile. "A merry heart doeth good like a medicine" (Proverbs 17:22).

4. Make eye contact immediately. Probably no other gesture signals your interest quite as much as this one.

5. If possible, call the other person by name.

6. The awkwardness of first contacts can be lessened by the realization that most people love to talk about themselves. A few sincere questions about someone's interests usually can get the ball of conversation rolling. Don't worry about what you can say. Just show a genuine interest in the other person's life.

7. As long as we sincerely are interested in people and believe in their essential worth, that concern will be reflected in our eyes, our facial expressions, as well as the tone of voice, and will draw people to us.

8. Everyone has some good points. Look for them and offer sincere compliments. Nothing turns off most people quite as rapidly as hollow, insincere remarks.

9. Remember that the world has an abundance of shy people who are just waiting for someone to come along and notice them.

10. Watch your body language. It has been said that in conversation we learn seven percent from the words themselves, 37 percent from the tone and inflection of the voice, and 56 percent from body language, especially the facial expressions. No one is going to believe we are very interested in her if we look over her shoulder at someone else, stare at the floor, glance at our watches, or look elsewhere while we are talking. If our face bears a frown or other unpleasant look instead of a smile, other people will not be attracted. We may not intend to appear uninterested or aloof, but that is the message our body language is emitting. It can be more powerful than any words from our mouths. Closed posture, such as crossing our arms, automatically carries with it the message, "I am shutting you out."

11. In all conversations, but especially in initial ones, we should guard our tongues and never talk about people in a degrading manner. If we criticize someone the first time we talk to new acquaintances, they undoubtedly will conclude that we probably will talk about them in the same manner as soon as their backs are turned. They certainly would not be hopeful about any potential for a real friendship.

12. Be a good listener. Lean forward. Pay attention to what the other person is saying instead of allowing your mind to race forward to your own next comment. You want the other person to receive the message, "You are important to me. I want to hear what you are saying."

13. Be willing to see the other person again if there is genuine interest between you, but don't exert pressure. Realize that one must allow time for friendships to grow. They cannot be forced any more than love.

"Wishing to be friends is quick work, but friendship a slow-ripening fruit." — Aristotle

Someone has said that when the chemistry of friendship takes, it is just as natural as the purring of a kitten. This comment is true, but the initial contact is vital. Someone else may look at your dearest friend and think, "I wouldn't want her for a close friend at all." But she's right for you.

The attraction must be right for real friendship to develop, but we certainly should be aware of the importance of those first contacts.

Seed #5: Be Genuine

If we are completely honest, most of us would have to admit to wearing protective masks at one time or another.

The reasons for hiding behind facades are myriad. Some believe people will be attracted to them only when they themselves appear to be perfect or only if they have an outstanding list of achievements. They concentrate upon presenting a superior image to other people. People may admire us for our achievements, but admiration is not friendship. Most of us even feel a bit uncomfortable when we are around someone who has her act together because it makes us feel inferior.

Some may be afraid to expose themselves for fear of rejection. They believe that if their true personality is revealed, people no longer will like them. Quite to the contrary, most of us instinctively are drawn closer to an individual who is a real person, to someone who is transparent and who is not ashamed to stand before us as she really is, warts and all. We can identify with people who are big enough to admit their humanity probably because it makes us feel better to realize that we ourselves do not have to be perfect to be accepted.

To bear the constant weight of a mask we are afraid to remove is emotionally tiring. A wonderful freedom accompanies the ability to be the same kind of person each day of our lives, wherever we are.

Christ gave us a perfect example of being genuine. As He daily traveled with His band of followers, they saw His tears (Luke 19:41; John 11:35), His anger (Mark 3:5), His frustrations (Luke 6:46), His disappointments (Luke 22:61), as well as His love (John 15:13).

Joseph Newton observed that people are lonely because they build walls instead of bridges. Being transparent provides a very effective bridge into the lives of people.

Disclosures of ourselves occur in different stages. Our conversations grow from facts to opinions to true feelings. Although revealing our deepest thoughts to everyone we meet is not advisable, a sense of freedom comes with being able to be ourselves wherever we are, without layers of pretense. Even more wonderful is believing we have a few close friends with whom we can stand emotionally naked and share our innermost feelings. As long as we have at least one friend to whom we can bare our inner core, we can make it through practically anything life sends our way.

Marian Evans (George Eliot) expressed the freedom that comes from being ourselves with these words:

> "Oh the comfort, the inexpressible comfort of feeling safe with a person; having neither to weigh thoughts nor measure words but to pour them all out, just as it is, chaff and grain together, knowing that a faithful hand will take and sift them, keeping what is worth keeping, and then, with the breath of kindness, blow the rest away."

Seed #6: Accept the Uniqueness of Other People

If friendship is ever to develop, some common interests must be shared or else the relationship would never leave the acquaintance stage. We enjoy engaging in activities with certain people and derive pleasure from the viewpoints we share. Similarities constitute the glue that binds people together in the first place.

No two people are alike in every respect. Not too much time elapses before we discover that our friends have some qualities we do not share and perhaps may even find a bit irritating. The person with whom we share many wonderful events and viewpoints may happen to be our opposite in other respects. Suppose, for example, that we pride ourselves on our promptness, both in arriving on time and in taking care of our affairs. Our friend, on the other hand, is nearly always late and never handles any business until she is pushed into a corner by a pressing deadline.

If the friendship is to continue to grow, we should realize that we cannot remake everyone into our own image. In fact, the world would be very dull if everyone were carbon copies of ourselves. We must learn to accept the uniqueness of individuals and give them the freedom to be themselves while we realize that differences add spice to life. The rainbow of contrasting traits makes life beautiful.

"If a man does not keep pace with his companions, perhaps it is because he hears a different drummer. Let him step to the music he hears, however measured and far away." — Henry David Thoreau

Acceptance does not carry with it the idea of approval. A friend loves at all times (Proverbs 17:17), but nothing was ever mentioned about liking someone all the time. The annoying habits of our friends may get on our nerves, but we must remember that our corresponding traits could be equally annoying to them. For example, there is nothing that drives a messy person to despair more easily than a neatnik. The same principle applies to the conflict between punctual and tardy individuals. We simply must accept the fact that we are different. If a friendship is to be successful, both persons should have breathing room.

"My friend is not perfect — no more than I — and so we suit each other admirably." — Alexander Pope

Consider the uniqueness of the friends of Christ. Matthew, the despised tax collector, was chosen by the Lord. Peter, the impulsive one who characteristically acted first and then thought, was loved by Jesus and was given the opportunity to put his impetuousness to good use on the Day of Pentecost. The quibbling about greatness in the kingdom by the two brothers, James and John, must have been annoying, but Christ loved them anyway.

Perhaps the main thrust of accepting the uniqueness of other people is best summarized in the words of Thoreau: "Friends do not live in harmony, merely, as some say, but in melody." May we accept our different notes as blending in a beautiful melody.

The distinction must be made between a unique trait that borders on annoyance and an attribute that is morally wrong. Whether an individual picks up her clothes or is ever on time has nothing to do with her salvation. On the other hand, her differing trait could be classified as sin in God's sight. Are we to remain complacent concerning such critical issues? Would we want our friend to be lost eternally because of the way she is living? Certainly not. It would be our responsibility to try, gently and lovingly, to guide her to realize the foolishness of her actions. Differences in personalities, however, we leave alone.

Conclusion

If the soil is right, throughout life we will reap a garden of diversified plants when we sow seeds of friendship by:
   (1) developing a proper perspective of other people;
   (2) making people a priority;
   (3) circulating;
   (4) taking the initiative in reaching out;
   (5) being genuine; and
   (6) accepting the uniqueness of people.

Questions

1. Is it wrong to seek friendships to lessen our own loneliness? What should be our primary reasons?
2. Why should our friendship with God (as well as with our ourselves) be right before we seek the friendship of other people?
3. If we go through life scattering the seeds of friendship, will the seeds always produce friends? Why?
4. Think back over the friends in your lifetime. Has the diversity of the relationships been a burden in your life or a blessing? Give some examples.
5. Relate Galatians 6:7 and 2 Corinthians 9:6 to this part of the study.
6. How does our perception of people influence our actions as well as the actions of other people?

7. If we generally perceive of people as being good, warm and loving, how do we treat them? What are the results when we believe someone will hurt us? Is that good or bad?

8. Why is it necessary to make people a priority in life? What are some of the rituals of friendship? Are they important? Why?

9. Common sense tells us that many potential friendships remain undeveloped because we do not make the effort to circulate among a wide variety of people. What are some of our self-imposed walls that isolate us from other people?

10. What are some ways in which we can create an environment that is conducive to the growth of possible friendships?

11. Someone must take the initiative in developing each friendship. Who is hurt the most if we always wait for the other person to take the lead?

12. Discuss the implications for friendship in these two passages: Proverbs 18:24 and Matthew 7:12.

13. Discuss the 13 suggestions made for reaching out during the burgeoning stages of friendship. Add the measures that have brought you success.

14. Discuss these two reasons for hiding behind protective masks: (1) People will like us only if we have many achievements and are nearly perfect in everything we do, and (2) people will reject us if they see the real person.

15. Why do we seem to be drawn instinctively to a person who is genuine? Can any of us say we are always completely transparent?

16. Discuss these passages to show that Christ revealed a wide range of emotions: Luke 19:41; John 11:35; Mark 3:5; Luke 6:46; Luke 22:61; John 15:13.

17. Did the followers of Christ ever really understand Him? Whose fault was it?

18. How can we deal with some of our friends' characteristics that may be annoying to us? Give some examples from your circle of friends. What happens when we try to make people over?

19. Does acceptance mean approval? What is the difference between an annoying trait and an attribute that is morally wrong?

20. Does loving someone mean we like her all the time?
21. Discuss the uniqueness of the friends of Christ. Did He love them all the time? Did He ever rebuke them?
22. Summarize the six seeds of friendship discussed in this chapter.

The Seeds of Friendship, Pt. 2

Seed #7: Look for the Good, and Express Your Appreciation

Each of us is a mixture of good and bad. At times one must gently, but firmly, rebuke a friend. However, most of us can be elevated to higher levels of action by honest, sincere praise and appreciation. William James, a pioneer of American psychology, very wisely observed, "The deepest principle in human nature is the craving to be appreciated."

This strong need for appreciation and approval can result in two divergent manifestations. Seeking acceptance has been responsible for the downfall of many, especially young people, who so desperately crave the approval of their peers that they even commit crimes to feel acceptance. On the other hand, countless other people have been encouraged to improve because someone believed in them and paved the way for achievement.

Luke has admonished us to treat other people the way we would like to be treated (Luke 6:31). We all want to be loved and appreciated. If we fulfill this basic longing in other people, our actions can go far in helping them reach their potential while we build lasting friendships.

We often attend funerals and hear about many wonderful attributes of the deceased person as friends talk with one another. How sad when we find the good things to say about someone only at the time of death, having failed to mention words of praise while the person was living. Kind words spoken over a casket are too late.

For 17 years I taught first graders in the public school system. My daily practice was to select a class leader to be my special person for the day. As the special student leader sat before the group, each member of the class was encouraged to say one good thing about the child. Nothing negative was permitted; only positive comments were allowed. In the process, the youngster's confidence was built up, and the other children gained skills in looking for the good in people instead of dwelling on the bad.

Children who have been reared in positive, expressive homes find it easy to express good feelings, but this character quality can be developed in anyone.

Another lesson learned during those teaching years was the power of praise in changing lives. It was much easier to change a negative trait by watching the individual and lavishly praising him whenever I noticed he was doing the right thing. This approach was far more effective than simply criticizing the negative.

Looking for the good in others trains the eyes of the heart until we soon become quite skilled in finding the nuggets of good in everyone.

Christ walked through the regions of Palestine, seeing the good in people and telling them about His belief in them. He apparently saw the potential for good in Zacchaeus, the Samaritan woman at the well, Mary Magdalene, and countless others. His belief in them and His encouragement fulfilled a basic need in each of them and made them open to His teachings.

First Corinthians 13:4 tells us that love is kind. Kindness looks for ways to build up people. In Ephesians 4:32 Paul admonished the early Christians to be kind to one another. Romans 16 is filled with Paul's open praise for so many of his coworkers as he mentioned the special contributions of each one.

Today we are far removed from Christ's time on earth and from the first-century epistles. How well have we incorporated these principles into our lives? When was the last time you wrote a note of appreciation to the preacher for a special lesson? To a new convert, welcoming him into the family of God? To your child's school-teacher, who went the second mile in her responsibilities? To your parents, thanking them for all the sacrifices they have made for you? To someone who thoughtfully performed some act of service that was especially meaningful to you when you were sick? To a child-hood friend who positively influenced your life? To friends who no longer live near you but who still have a special place in your heart? Have we told many people how much they mean to us? Why do we find it difficult to express our appreciation? If it is difficult to say, "I love you," can we perhaps manage to utter, "I've missed you" or "Your friendship means so much to me"?

Make it a practice to find something praiseworthy in each person you meet. Sincerely tell everyone how much you appreciate an ad-mirable trait in him or her. Soon offering such praise will become a way of life. Remember that our affirmation must be sincere. Nothing rings quite as hollow as insincerity.

Seed #8: Sow the Seed of Unselfishness Throughout Life

Friendship leaves no room for selfishness. Love does not seek her own (1 Corinthians 13:5). John 15:13 goes a step further, asserting, "Greater love hath no man than this, that a man lay down his life for his friends." While we probably will not be called upon to give up our own lives for our friends, we certainly should be willing to give of our time, energy and personal possessions to help if a need aris-es. Sometimes a lifetime devoted to the giving of ourselves to oth-er people is even more demanding than a one-time act of sacrific-ing our very lives for a friend.

Within the pages of the Scriptures we find some examples of unselfish love. Beginning in 1 Samuel 18 is the story of true friend-ship between two men, David and Jonathan. As the son of King Saul, Jonathan was the logical heir to the throne of Israel, but God had other plans. In His divine wisdom, He selected David, a common shepherd boy, to assume the place of leadership. Jonathan sacrificed his own future by protecting and defending his friend David. The son of Saul gave up his own right to the throne because he loved David and respected God's will. What a great example of unselfish friendship this story teaches!

God and Christ constitute the supreme examples of sacrificial love. "For God so loved the world, that he gave his only begotten Son, that whosoever believeth in him should not perish, but have everlasting life" (John 3:16). I doubt that any of us would offer the life of one of our own children for the benefit of anyone else. But God did! Christ Himself loved us enough to give up His own life for each of us in the supreme sacrifice.

Another example of unselfishness may be found in Acts. The early church was composed of Jews from many different nations. Such a large group of people, who elected to remain in a foreign city, constituted an emergency. They needed food and other necessities of life while they were away from home. In order to alleviate this problem, the early Christians sold their possessions and shared with one another (Acts 4:32). What an unselfish attitude these people displayed!

Selfishness sparks jealousy. Sometimes our eyes grow a bit green with envy when a friend achieves an honor or gains in earthly possessions. As long as she was down and out, we were her friend because she needed us. Now that she is standing on her own two feet and even has something we secretly wish we could have, we think she no longer needs us. We don't like to admit it, but we are envious. How often do we have the same attitude as that of the older brother in Luke 15:29? "And he answering said to his father, Lo, these many years do I serve thee, neither transgressed I at any time thy commandment: and yet thou never gavest me a kid, that I might make merry with my friends."

Unselfishness simply means that we think of other people instead of ourselves and do everything we can to help them succeed in life. It may seem paradoxical, but when we help people succeed, we discover that we ourselves have found what is really important in life. The magnet of unselfishness attracts people to us.

Seed #9: Allow Space in Your Friendships

The fundamental principle of space is based upon the seed of unselfishness. Friendship has no room for possessiveness. Expecting a friend to have no other friends nor outside interests is nothing but selfishness. People cannot be treated as private property.

The person who can stand on her own two feet usually makes the best friend. She does not find it necessary to have people depending on her for her own sense of worth. Having friendships with a number of people herself and allowing her friends to enjoy relationships with other people is a sign of maturity.

A friendship that has the potential for being warm and flourishing can be smothered if one of the partners demands practically all the time and attention of the other. Solomon warned about this fault when he wrote, "Withdraw thy foot from thy neighbor's house; lest he be weary of thee, and so hate thee" (Proverbs 25:17). If we are perfectly honest, most of us can identify with this verse. At least one person in our lives would have made a wonderful friend if we could have had her in smaller doses. Instead, she camped out on our doorstep or called each day. Whenever we tried to engage in an activity with another person, she became very jealous.

We should want what is best for our friends as well as for ourselves. Each of us is composed of bits and pieces of every person who has ever touched our lives, and we become a more complete person by interacting in the lives of many because strength comes from a network of friends. No one person can supply all our friendship needs.

The ropes binding friendship should be tight enough to hold it together but flexible enough to allow for space in the relationship. We all must have the freedom to be our own selves instead of just being a part of another person. For years I have enjoyed the thoughts of an unknown writer: "If you love someone, set him free. If he returns to you, he's yours forever. If he doesn't, he was never yours in the first place."

Sometimes we need space in a friendship in order to strengthen our relationships with other people. At times we need our space simply to be alone. How can I offer my friendship to you if I have never taken the time to understand just who I am? We all need time to be by ourselves in addition to some silence while we are in the presence of a friend.

Sometimes people try to manipulate others by acting superior to them rather than setting them free. People may admire us for our accomplishments, but they will not love us for them. At other times some may endeavor to control people around them by acting helpless. For example, a selfish mother may keep the apron strings tied securely to her adult child by using her own poor health as an excuse for refusing to let go. Still other women do not set their friends free simply because they have such an overwhelming desire to be needed themselves.

If we love our friends, we should want what is best for them. They need to stand on their own two feet and develop their own potential to the fullest. They need a number of friends for support throughout life, and we should encourage them to be independent.

Remember that friendship loves free air and survives best when each person has developed her own network of friends.

Seed #10: Don't Keep Score

Many times you've heard someone complain, "I wrote Mary, but she still hasn't answered my letter." "I telephoned Mindy and she never returned my call." "We had Bill and Sue over for a meal last. They haven't invited us into their home for several months." "I sent Pam a card for her birthday, but she didn't remember mine."

We must remember we are dealing with imperfect people who have nearly as many faults as we have. Folks usually mean well, but they often forget or simply procrastinate. Most of it is caused by thoughtlessness.

As long as we derive pleasure in being with another person and in doing little things to make her happy, forget about who did what last. It's really not that important. Instead, we should be grateful for anything we receive and should give for the joy of giving. If we expect perfection from other people, we will be disappointed. It is better to realize that we, too, have our own faults, which we want to be understood and tolerated.

"When befriended, remember it. When you befriend, forget it." — Franklin

Seed #11: Practice the Gestures of Friendship Automatically

Love is far more than a feeling or emotion. Love is something we do for other people. As we search constantly for ways to enrich the lives of people around us, we gradually develop a mind-set that senses their needs and desires. We automatically respond without consciously thinking of our actions. Layer by layer, various acts of kindness accumulate until they assume the strength of lacquered wood. One loving gesture after another bonds two people together and prevents the breaking apart of a relationship during the natural ebb and flow of emotions.

"We cannot tell the precise moment when friendship is formed. As in filling a vessel drop by drop, there is at last a drop which makes it run over; so in a series of kindnesses there is at last one that makes the heart run over." — James Boswell

The gestures of friendship assume many different forms: spoken words, written messages, shared social activities, service to people, eating together, and giving gifts, to name but a few.

1. Spoken words form the basis of many gestures of friendship. Sincerely complimenting someone about something she has done well is important, and passing on compliments heard from other people is even more meaningful.

A brief telephone call offering congratulations or concern means much, too. A daily call to check on the physical condition of an elderly neighbor to see if you can be of help is a great way to show your concern. I can well remember that my mother and a neighbor talked over the telephone every morning right after breakfast — a ritual of friendship that lasted for years. Naturally, the daily conversations bonded the two women.

When was the last time you called a friend who lives some distance from you? Perhaps you had not seen her in several years, but the first few minutes of sharing your lives once again made you realize how very much she has meant to you. Telephone rates are very competitive, lessening the cost of keeping in touch.

2. Written words lack the benefit of eye contact, but they have the advantage of permanence. Birthday cards, accompanied by a personal message and exchanged between dear friends for many years, are valuable in keeping in touch across the miles. Spontaneous notes for no special occasion speak a caring message all their own. When was the last time you wrote a letter to a longtime friend, telling her how much she has meant to your life and what a positive influence she has been? Every such note I receive is reread many times and eventually goes into my special "Friends Box" on the top closet shelf for reading on gloomy days.

3. Shared social activities often become rituals of friendship. Excursions to ball games, tennis matches, jogging, walking, and other such events provide the cement for bonding two people together. Yearly, or even monthly, shopping trips also help cement relationships. While the men in the family take care of the children, my daughter and I go shopping the day after Thanksgiving. We enjoy lunch together and having the time to shop. It has become a family ritual.

4. Activities of service not only bond the participants together in friendship but also draw close to them those who are being served. Taking meals to someone who is sick, for example, can lead to the bonding of several people. As we become more watchful and open to the needs of other people, we will find many avenues of service: caring for sick children, staying by the bedside of people in the hospital, taking food and groceries to people in need. The list is endless.

5. So many of our gestures of friendship center around the act of eating together. Passage after passage relating to the life of Jesus finds the Master sharing a meal with friends. He daily ate with His apostles. He frequently was in the home of Mary, Martha and Lazarus. Christ also attended various feasts throughout His ministry.

In our modern-day setting, something significant happens when we put our feet under the same table with friends and talk face to face. Daily luncheons shared with a fellow worker, a monthly luncheon date with a friend, the sharing of birthday celebrations, and meals together in one another's homes are special rituals of friendship.

6. Giving gifts also is a gesture of friendship. The scriptural account of David and Jonathan is an excellent example of the significance of gifts. The son of Jesse and the son of King Saul made a covenant and sealed it by the giving of Jonathan's robe, sword, bow and girdle to David (1 Samuel 18:1-4).

Gifts do not need to be expensive. Some of the most meaningful ones are simple things purchased for a friend who casually mentioned she would like to have them. Others simply can be called gifts of the heart. They are unexpected presents given as a means of transmitting love and caring concern from one heart to another. That love could be embodied in a bud vase of flowers personally delivered to a shut-in or a bottle of lotion taken to a longtime resident of the nursing home who hopes someone might take the time to visit her that day.

"A gift is as a precious stone in the eyes of him that hath it: whithersoever it turneth, it prospereth" (Proverbs 17:8).

"Withhold not good from them to whom it is due, when it is in the power of thine hand to do it" (Proverbs 3:27).

Never take friendship for granted. It must be nurtured and repaired constantly. A bond is created by the giving and receiving of gifts as a feeling of closeness flows from the giver to the receiver and back to the giver.

Seed #12: Allow People to Do Things for You

At first glance these words may seem paradoxical. Isn't the building of better relationships supposed to be based upon doing things for people? Shouldn't we be independent? Why should we allow people to give of themselves to us?

Although it is more blessed to give than to receive (Acts 20:35), it is also vital to let your friends know you need them and to accept gestures of friendship from them. Allowing people to do a favor for you helps to cement the bond of friendship. Just as it makes us feel good to do things for our friends, it is also true that they receive enjoyment from doing special things for us.

Sometimes it is difficult to say a simple thank-you to one who has extended a gesture of friendship to us, but it is bad for a relationship when the same person is always in the superior position of being the giver. We all feel better about ourselves when we can step into the benefactor's position from time to time. There must be a balance. Asking a friend to do a favor for you can be a source of strength to the relationship, but doing so never should be abused or unreasonable.

How many times have we brushed off a sincere compliment with a comment like, "Oh, this old thing? I've had it for years." Have you ever given a gift and barely received an acknowledgement of it, much less any heartfelt thanks? How did that make you feel? How do you think people feel when they receive the same treatment from you? To downplay any gestures of friendship from someone is tantamount to a slap in the face.

Christ gave of Himself freely as He and the apostles traveled together for three years, but He also graciously accepted gifts as a divine being in a human body. As a baby, Jesus received the expensive gifts from the wise men. The woman who anointed Him with ointment used a costly gift to show her devotion. The Samaritan woman drew water for our Lord. Mary and Martha, along with others, prepared meals for Him. A group of women followed this itinerant preacher and His band of followers from Galilee throughout Judea, ministering to them. Jesus would not even have had a place for His burial were it not for the generosity of Joseph of Arimathea. From the days of His birth through the time of His burial, Christ, our supreme example, freely gave of Himself and graciously accepted gifts of love.

We should be mature enough to realize that people feel gratified when they do something special for us. May we accept their gestures of friendship with love. May we also remember the gratitude we experience from receiving and promise ourselves that we never will neglect this meaningful part of friendship.

One special gift that I will never forget was given to me a number of years ago. One of my first-grade students was having difficulty mastering the academics for that grade level. The pupil, his parents and I had worked hard all year long. As the year neared the end, we had another conference and mutually decided it would be far wiser for the child to repeat the grade and get a better foundation than to promote him into future failure. The last day of school, the boy came to me with something clutched in his hand and said he had a present for me. He placed in my hand his well-used little car. Through the years I have kept that gift. The scratched, worn car was symbolic of his feelings that day. It said, "I love you, and it's OK."

Remember that the joy we receive from a gift is not so much the gift itself but another's love in giving it.

Conclusion

Let's review the six seeds of friendship discussed in the previous chapter:

1. Develop a proper perspective of other people.
2. Make people a priority.
3. Circulate among people.
4. Take the initiative in reaching out.
5. Be genuine.
6. Accept the uniqueness of other people.

This chapter added these seeds to the list:

7. Look for the good, and express your appreciation.
8. Sow the seed of unselfishness throughout life.
9. Allow space in your friendships.
10. Don't keep score.
11. Practice the gestures of friendship automatically.
12. Allow people to do things for you.

Questions

1. Why is the desire for praise and appreciation so vital?
2. How can the fulfilling of this need be both good and bad? Read Luke 6:31 and apply the principle.
3. Do you believe an unfavorable trait may be changed for the better by criticism or by praise when the person is doing something right? Is there a place for both?

4. Jesus looked for the good in Zacchaeus, the Samaritan woman at the well, and Mary Magdalene. Discuss the instances and add others.

5. Paul mentioned many workers by name in Romans 16. Discuss Paul's treatment of them.

6. Name some people who would be uplifted by a note of appreciation from you. What do you plan to do about it?

7. What can we learn concerning unselfishness from 1 Corinthians 13:5 and John 15:13?

8. How did the friendship of David and Jonathan exhibit such great unselfishness?

9. To what degree did God and Christ display sacrificial love?

10. According to Acts 4:32, how did the early Christians show unselfishness?

11. How did the older brother in Luke 15:29 show selfishness? Was he justified?

12. Discuss Proverbs 25:17 and the principle of space in our relationships. Why are some people so possessive?

13. How can the practice of "keeping score" be detrimental to our relationships?

14. How can love be a feeling and an action?

15. How can acts of kindness bond two people?

16. Discuss the forms of these gestures of friendship: spoken words, written words, shared social activities, activities of service, eating together, and giving gifts.

17. Why is it sometimes difficult to allow people to do things for us? How can the practice strengthen a friendship?

18. Christ accepted gifts during His ministry. Discuss each of these instances, and add to the list: gifts from the wise men; the ointment from the woman who anointed Him; the drink of water from the Samaritan woman; meals prepared at the home of Mary, Martha and Lazarus; acts of kindness performed by the women who followed Jesus and the apostles from Galilee; and the burial place from Joseph of Arimathea.

CHAPTER 6

The Seeds of Friendship, Pt. 3

Seed #13: Be Committed to Your Friends

In long-lasting friendships, there must be commitment, or loyalty, to one another. Marriage, the most intimate of all relationships, is characterized by this bonding in a formal sense. In essence, at the wedding ceremony we are promising our mates that we will never forsake them. We will be with them though thick and thin, the times of joy as well as the periods of hardship. We promise to love them when they are unlovable because we have made a commitment. We realize that we ourselves will not always be lovable, and we want them to be there with us.

We easily can understand the necessity of a lifetime commitment to one another in marriage, but what about in our friendships?

Far too many people move constantly from one friendship to another while always blaming the other people for the troubles that develop. They believe the perfect friend must be somewhere. They constantly bicker with family members, and all too often they also move from one marriage partner to another. Such people never seem to realize that their lack of commitment is at the root of the trouble. They never have given friendship time to work out its problems. Each of us is imperfect. We must realize that friendship, like marriage, is going to have its ebb and flow. We must stick with it until we work out our disagreements.

A wonderful biblical account of commitment in friendship is given in the story of David and Jonathan, two friends who were bonded for life. The soul of Jonathan was knit with the soul of David, and Jonathan loved him as his own soul (1 Samuel 18:1). Jonathan realized that the common shepherd one day would be the ruler of the nation, which would deprive Jonathan himself of his rightful position as heir to King Saul's kingdom. Yet, the two young men had immense loyalty to one another.

Saul tried to destroy David for several years, but Jonathan stood by his friend, even risking his own life. "Then said Jonathan unto David, Whatsoever thy soul desireth, I will even do it for thee" (1 Samuel 20:4). Their commitment was sealed with the giving of symbolic gifts and took the form of a covenant (1 Samuel 18:3) — a covenant that extended to the next generation. After the deaths of King Saul and Jonathan, King David asked whether any descendants of the house of Saul still lived "that I may show him kindness for Jonathan's sake" (2 Samuel 9:1). Mephibosheth, the crippled son of Jonathan, was brought to the palace, where he ate at the royal table for the rest of his life (2 Samuel 9:1-13).

Lifetime friendships have a similar bond. Generally, no formal commitment is made, as in the example of David and Jonathan or in the exchanging of wedding vows, but an unwritten understanding is felt between two friends that they will be there for one another forever. The unspoken glue of commitment holds friends together while they are working out their differences. And the disagreements certainly will come!

Friends learn to trust one another at the beginning of the relationship. Layer upon layer, two people build their friendship on this foundation. When one tells the other something of a confidential nature, she holds those words in a sacred trust and repeats them to no one. Telling a confidence to a third party destroys the trust that has been established between friends. "A talebearer revealeth secrets: but he that is of a faithful spirit concealeth the matter" (Proverbs 11:13). The supreme test of loyalty is the willingness to lay down one's life for her friends (John 15:13).

Any friendship will experience times in which one person gives more than the other. Our generation, with its assertiveness and refusal to allow anyone to take advantage of us as we elbow our way to the front, is selfish. The happiest people are those who feel confidant of their own worth and do not need to brush other people aside in a quest for their rights. Instead, they have learned that their rewards come from helping others and contributing to their happiness. They also have learned that there are times when each friend does most of the giving.

"The most I can do for my friend is simply to be his friend."
— Henry David Thoreau

Seed #14: Try Stepping into the Other Person's Shoes

Much of the trouble that develops from relating with people can be summarized in one thought: We often experience misunderstandings and fail to accept other people simply because we do not take the time to try to understand how they feel.

Perhaps their actions are not right, and we need not condone them. However, we can accept the person, if not the actions, by walking in the other person's shoes for a few miles. We may see her outward harshness, irritability, indifference or aloofness while having no idea just what is going on in her mind. She may be trying to cope with some overwhelming problems that constitute an insurmountable stress load. We also probably would react negatively if we were facing those same problems.

Remember that love looks with the heart, not the eyes. Love sees something good in other people, despite all their shortcomings, and builds upon that foundation in bringing out the best in them. These words have been posted over my kitchen sink for a number of years, and they have meant a lot to me:

"Blessed are they who have the gift of making friends, for it is one of God's best gifts. It involves many things, but above all, the power of going out of one's self, and appreciating whatever is noble and loving in another." — Thomas Hughes

Seed #15: Take Time for Friendships

This is a busy world. In our culture, nearly every adult who is physically able has a job outside the home. We are in a mad rush all day long as we frantically dash out of the house in the morning, meet constant deadlines in our work, run several necessary errands on our way home, prepare and serve dinner, wash and dry clothes, do a little housework while helping our children with their homework, and then get the kids to bed before we ourselves finally collapse for the night, only to begin the same cycle over the next morning. We have been surrounded by people all day long, and yet we have had no time for any lasting friendships.

Friendships require time — time for more than just a few snatches of conversation, time for in-depth talking and sharing, time for laughter, time to drop everything and be there when needed. Lasting friendships are not made by flying together in flocks. There must be ample opportunities to be with people on a one-to-one basis. Each person's schedule is unique; only some serious soul searching can help us get our priorities straight and make time for what is important rather than just what is urgent.

Seed #16: Learn the Skills of Communication

Because a cornerstone of friendship involves the sharing of feelings, good communication is one of the most important seeds anyone can sow throughout life.

Thoughts pass from one person to another over three main bridges: our ears, our words and our body language. All are important and deserve more attention than we normally give them.

Sometimes we are overconcerned about being witty and having the right thing to say. These matters are really not terribly important. We ourselves are interesting when we are sincerely interested in the other person. The secret to initiating good conversation is our encouraging people to talk about themselves by asking them questions they will enjoy answering. While they are talking, we should not be thinking about what we will say in reply or how we can top what is being said with a more exciting story. Instead, we listen with an open heart as we absorb the feelings and intent of the one who is talking.

We listen with more than our ears. Our interest in people can be determined by the manner in which our bodies react to them. Do we look at someone else in the room while someone is talking to us? Do we stare over her shoulder? Do we fidget with our hands? Do we look at our watches? Or do we move closer and look intently into her eyes as she talks? Our body language can be powerful in letting the other person know we care about her and are genuinely interested in what she has to say.

We also gain much insight into the real meaning of people's words by their body language. We are observant of their tone of voice, their facial expressions, their eye contact, their tenseness, and their openness in expression. We listen with our hearts and eyes as well as with our ears.

While the skills of listening and being aware of body language are important, the third bridge of communication is vital: words. As the primary vehicles used to transport ideas from one person to another, words are important. Some people naturally are more reticent than others, and entering into conversations is extremely difficult for them. Other people are chatterboxes who seem to rattle effortlessly about trivia. Neither extreme is ideal.

If one person does all the talking and the other one never does anything but listen, then there is no dialogue, no sharing of ideas between two friends. At certain times, one will do more listening while the other does most of the talking, and sometimes the situation is reversed. In a balanced friendship both people share their thoughts by talking, and both take turns listening.

Sometimes we seem awkward in initiating conversations and don't know what to say. A certain amount of chit-chat is involved in getting the ball rolling, and a knowledge of what is going on in the world usually provides the stimulus for initiating the flow of ideas. Discussing similar interests and activities is good fuel for the fire of conversation. By expressing an interest in another's likes and dislikes, we encourage the other person to talk about herself.

Being sensitive to the feelings and needs of other people is the foundation for sharing thoughts with them. Our friends test us by telling us about themselves, little by little. If we seem to respect their thoughts and keep their confidences, they tend to expose more of their true feelings the next time we talk. Friendship is based upon trust. Whenever that trust is broken, the relationship suffers. Sometimes it can never be repaired.

We should be aware of our own body language as we talk. Is our facial expression a pleasant one or a scowl? Do we look the other person in the eye? Voice tone greatly influences the manner in which our words are interpreted. Are we animated and full of excitement, or does the tone of our voice project the idea of boredom?

Our own personalities are the most important factors in communicating with other people, and we must work within our natural framework. However, most of us can improve our body-language skills as well as our listening and speaking abilities with just a little thought and effort.

Good communication requires time, and in this busy world, spare moments are rare. Time for the sharing of ideas with one another requires planning. Husbands and wives, especially, need to set aside blocks of time, on a daily and a weekly basis, just for being with one another without interruption. The schedule of each household is unique, but time for communicating our likes, dislikes, hopes and fears should be made a priority.

In *Living Together in Knowledge*, the book co-written by my husband and me, we made several observations concerning good communication in marriage:

1. True communication must be a two-way street.
2. Realize that men and women are usually different in their expressiveness.
3. Good communication is impossible without trust.
4. Be sensitive to feelings.
5. Take time for communication.
6. Learn the language of communication.
7. Develop the art of listening.
8. Resolve irritations before they fester.

9. Realize that communication is intended for growth through problem solving instead of tearing the other person down.

10. Couples should first learn to talk honestly in nonthreatening areas before they can even attempt to explore one another's feelings on such subjects as fears, insecurities, jealousy, a new job, or moving to a new location.

11. No one has the right to attach motives to what another person says or does.

12. The basic element underlying all communication is love.

Practicing the skills of communication is vital in our relationships in the world, in our community, on our jobs, and in our homes.

Seed #17: Find the Nuggets of Gold in God's Word

The Scriptures abound with words of wisdom relating to friendship. In particular, the book of Proverbs, from which all the following passages come, is rich in admonitions concerning the use of the tongue and the power of words.

The right words have great benefits.

"A word fitly spoken is like apples of gold in pictures of silver" (25:11).

"Pleasant words are as an honeycomb, sweet to the soul, and health to the bones" (16:24).

"By long forbearing is a prince persuaded, and a soft tongue breaketh the bone" (25:15).

"The wise in heart shall be called prudent: and the sweetness of the lips increaseth learning" (16:21).

"The heart of the wise teacheth his mouth, and addeth learning to his lips" (16:23).

"The tongue of the wise useth knowledge aright: but the mouth of fools poureth out foolishness" (15:2).

"A man hath joy by the answer of his mouth: and a word spoken in due season, how good is it!" (15:23).

Be wise in selecting your associates.

"Make no friendship with an angry man; and with a furious man thou shalt not go" (22:24).

"Be not thou envious against evil men, neither desire to be with them. For their heart studieth destruction, and their lips talk of mischief" (24:1-2).

"Put away from thee a froward mouth, and perverse lips put far from thee" (4:24).

"Eat thou not the bread of him that hath an evil eye, neither desire thou his dainty meats: For as he thinketh in his heart, so is he" (23:6-7).

Never underestimate the harm that words can cause.

"An hypocrite with his mouth destroyeth his neighbor" (11:9).

"A froward man soweth strife: and a whisperer separateth chief friends" (16:28).

Think before you speak.

"Seest thou a man that is hasty is his words? there is more hope of a fool than of him" (29:20).

There is a time and a place for even good things.

"He that blesseth his friend with a loud voice, rising early in the morning, it shall be counted a curse to him" (27:14).

Be careful what you say. Sometimes it is better to say nothing.

"Even a fool, when he holdeth his peace, is counted wise: and he that shutteth his lips is esteemed a man of understanding" (17:28).

"A fool's mouth is his destruction, and his lips are the snare of his soul" (18:7).

"Whoso keepeth his mouth and his tongue keepeth his soul from troubles" (21:23).

"He that keepeth his mouth keepeth his life: but he that openeth wide his lips shall have destruction" (13:3).

"A fool uttereth all his mind: but a wise man keepeth it in till afterwards" (29:11).

Talebearers reveal confidences and do great harm.

"The words of a talebearer are as wounds, and they go down into the innermost parts of the belly" (18:8; 26:22).

"Where no wood is, there the fire goeth out: so where there is no talebearer, the strife ceaseth" (26:20).

"He that hideth hatred with lying lips, and he that uttereth a slander, is a fool" (10:18).

"He that goeth about as a talebearer revealeth secrets: therefore meddle not with him that flattereth with his lips" (20:19).

Angry words can ruin relationships.

"A soft answer turneth away wrath: but grievous words stir up anger" (15:1).

"A wrathful man stirreth up strife: but he that is slow to anger appeaseth strife" (15:18).

"He that is slow to wrath is of great understanding: but he that is hasty of spirit exalteth folly" (14:29).

"As coals are to burning coals, and wood to fire; so is a contentious man to kindle strife" (26:21).

Look for ways to do good.

"Withhold not good from them to whom it is due" (3:27).

Cheerfulness comes from the heart.

"A merry heart maketh a cheerful countenance" (15:13).

The best way to have friends is to be friendly.

"A man that hath friends must show himself friendly" (18:24).

Do not wear out your welcome at a friend's house.
"Withdraw thy foot from thy neighbor's house; lest he be weary of thee, and so hate thee" (25:17).

Make your words appropriate for the occasion.
"As he that taketh away a garment in cold weather, and as vinegar upon nitre, so is he that singeth songs to a heavy heart" (25:20).

The Scriptures abound with principles for guiding our relationships, but they probably all can be summarized by the lessons taught in Matthew 7:12 and 22:34-40: Begin in your heart. Make God the first love of your life; then love your neighbor as yourself. Let your actions be natural extensions of the love in your heart by treating others the way you would like to be treated.

Conclusion

The previous two chapters suggested that these seeds of friendship be sown as we journey through life:

1. Develop a proper perspective of other people.
2. Make people a priority.
3. Circulate among people.
4. Take the initiative in reaching out.
5. Be genuine.
6. Accept the uniqueness of other people.
7. Look for the good, and express your appreciation.
8. Sow the seed of unselfishness throughout life.
9. Allow space in your friendships.
10. Don't keep score.
11. Practice the gestures of friendship automatically.
12. Allow people to do things for you.

This chapter adds five more seeds:

13. Be committed to your friends.
14. Try stepping into the other person's shoes.
15. Take time for friendships.
16. Learn the skills of communication.
17. Find the nuggets of gold in God's Word.

Questions

1. Discuss the importance of commitment to the marriage relationship.
2. What sort of commitment did David and Jonathan have? Do you think it was necessary?
3. Ideally, what sort of commitment should be at the foundation of a friendship?
4. What does the repeating of a confidence do to a friendship? Discuss Proverbs 11:13.
5. Why is a friendship not always an equal partnership in giving? Is this bad?
6. Why is it so difficult to understand how other people feel? How important is it?
7. How can we find the time needed for friendships in our hectic world?
8. We communicate to one another over three main bridges: our ears, our words and our body language. Discuss the strengths and weaknesses of each.
9. Discuss the suggestions for improving communication in the marriage relationship. Add to the list.
10. Relate these eternal Proverbs from God's Word as they pertain to the power of words:
    a. The right words have great benefits (25:11; 16:24; 25:15; 16:21, 23; 15:2, 23).
    b. Be wise in selecting your associates (22:24; 24:1-2; 4:24; 23:6-7).
    c. Never underestimate the harm that words can cause (11:9; 16:28).
    d. Think before you speak (29:20).
    e. There is a time and a place for even good things (27:14).
    f. Be careful what you say. Sometimes it is better to say nothing (17:28; 18:7; 21:23; 13:3; 29:11).
    g. Talebearers reveal confidences and do great harm (18:8; 26:20; 10:18; 20:19).

     h. Angry words can ruin our relationships with people (15:1, 18; 14:29; 26:21).

     i. Look for ways to do good (3:27).

     j. Cheerfulness comes from the heart (15:13).

     k. The best way to have friends is to be friendly (18:24).

     l. Do not wear out your welcome at a friend's house (25:17).

     m. Make your words appropriate for the occasion (25:20).

11. Search the Scriptures for more eternal truths that relate to the establishment and maintenance of friendships.

12. Summarize the messages from Matthew 7:12 and Matthew 22:34-40.

13. Summarize the material from the previous three chapters by evaluating the 17 seeds of friendship. Add your own suggestions.

CHAPTER 7

Friendship Between Husband and Wife

Probably no other relationship has the wide range of potentiality as the one found within the marriage union. Properly cultivated marital ground has the possibility of producing a kind of friendship that is unsurpassed by any other relationship. It also has the potential for developing distrust, selfishness and even hatred as two people live together under the same roof in the glaring light of daily routine.

God never intended for marriage to be a test of endurance, but rather a relationship in which the deepest needs of both man and woman can be fulfilled. At the time of Creation, again and again is found the phrase "And God saw that it was good." All was good, that is, until the creation of man. After Adam was placed over the care of the Garden of Eden, Jehovah decided it was not good for man to be alone, so a suitable helper was made in the form of Eve (Genesis 2:18, 21-22). Adam not only needed Eve in a physical sense, but he also needed her emotionally. For some, a life of solitude can eat at the very core of a human being until all usefulness is destroyed. How wonderful it is when husband and wife not only can blot out loneliness for one another but also can become best friends!

Dating Days

Boy meets girl. They are physically attracted to one another at a time in their lives when hormones are pouring into their bloodstreams.

Physical attraction is enhanced by the fact that limited time is spent with one another, and each one tries to put his or her best foot forward. Most people seem to be attracted by those whose personality strengths offset their own weaknesses. Love is often blind and usually sees only the needed complementary strengths in the date's good side while seeming to be oblivious to any weaknesses.

Each feeling that the perfect partner has been found, the bride and groom stand before witnesses in all the glitter of a wedding and vow to live together for the rest of their lives. In actuality, they scarcely even know the other person standing beside them. Their friendship with one another is only superficial at this time and will require several years before developing to the "best friends" level.

The soft, romantic honeymoon days soon settle into the glare of the real world. The daily grind — going to work, running a household, and pacing the floor at night with a crying baby — has a way of exposing the weaker side of our personalities. If the marriage is to last, and if it is to develop into a deep and lasting friendship between husband and wife, then there must be a lot of understanding and adjusting by both partners.

We Marry Three People

We may think we know the person who is standing by our side as we make our marriage vows, but we have only begun to scratch the surface. Hidden within the personality of the bride and groom is the child who is locked within the heart of each one. Early childhood usually colors a person's perception of life. One who is reared in a strict home will have a different outlook from one who has been brought up in a more permissive atmosphere. Moral teachings, religious training, and love (or lack of it) all leave their marks for good or for bad. Even family customs shape the child. Your mate is composed of countless layers of daily living that transpired before the two of you ever met.

The second person who lives within the body of the bride or groom is the older person who will eventually develop as the years go by. We all change with the passing of time. You are not the same person you were 10 years ago, and neither am I. We change — for better or for worse — with every new thought that enters our minds, through encounters with each person who is a significant part of our lives, with every verse of God's Word that is absorbed into our hearts, and with every good or bad experience. Poor health also takes its toll. After the children have left home, husbands and wives frequently find themselves living as two strangers under the same roof. The key to living happily with the person yet to come is daily adjustment to one another throughout the years.

The third and most evident person standing at the marriage altar is the bride or groom as he or she appears at that moment. We have been so enamored with the love of our lives that we have seen only the strengths, which normally seem to supply whatever is lacking in our own lives. The weaknesses are there, but we have been so blinded by love that we have not yet really noticed the negative. It is only normal to be different. We just have to put forth the effort to understand one another and accept those differences.

When we say, "I do," we are pledging our loyalty to the hidden child of years past, the older person yet to develop, and the complex individual standing by our side at that moment. Seldom do the bride and groom realize the awesome responsibility they are undertaking.

Differences in Temperaments

Locked within each person is his or her own inherited temperament, composed of inborn traits determined by the parents' genes and chromosomes at the moment of conception. Although the temperament can be modified for good or for bad by external factors, the basic core remains the same throughout life. Basically, it cannot be changed — only understood. The rough edges can be smoothed and channeled into a useful, productive life, but we must accept our mate's personality unconditionally.

In effect, with the pledging of love and devotion, the bride and groom are saying they feel secure enough to reveal themselves totally to one another, emotionally as well as physically, trusting that each will love the other just the same, despite weaknesses. Emotional nakedness can be more painful to endure than physical exposure.

Without consciously realizing the reasons, we are generally attracted to the temperament that most complements our own instead of being drawn to someone with similar traits. The fun-loving life of the party is seldom attracted to someone like himself. He needs an appreciative audience, which is usually found in one who is passive and does not desire the spotlight. The hard-driving, aggressive leader needs an easy-going follower. The unorganized person, who can never find anything, subconsciously yearns for someone to balance the checkbook and bring order to his life. The goof-off loves one who measures life by the amount of work accomplished. The person who enjoys picking a fight inevitably marries the peacemaker. On and on the list could go.

Temperaments are to be understood as variations in human nature. The happy couple focuses on one another's strengths while minimizing the weaknesses. It is all right to be different. In fact, it can be stimulating as long as the differences are understood. In reference to the idiosyncrasies of basic temperaments, it is wrong to constantly criticize those who are different from ourselves and try to change them. An introvert can be just as dedicated to serving the Lord as an extrovert. A messy, unorganized person can be just as valuable in the Lord's kingdom as someone who has a place for everything and everything in its place. In the long run, a night owl gets just as much work done as an early riser. A penny pincher and a spendthrift can bring balance to a marriage if they understand and cooperate.

We are happiest in life when we understand human temperaments instead of allowing them to grate on our nerves. Temperamental differences are wonderful! They attracted us to our mates in the first place. Be thankful for the strengths and accept the weaknesses; they add color to our lives.

Male-Female Differences

Individuals differ from one another due to inborn temperaments. Even more unique are the opposite traits often found in males and females. Aside from the more obvious sexual differences are many other ways in which men and women are not alike.

Physically, the hormones differ. A woman has fewer red blood cells than a man and, consequently, tires more easily. Men and women differ in the combination pattern of their chromosomes. A man's metabolism is higher. His lungs are larger, making his breathing capacity greater. He has more muscle tissue and is the stronger sex. On the other hand, a woman has greater constitutional vitality than a man and, in this country, normally outlives him by three or four years.

The emotional differences, however, play an even more important role in the harmony of a marriage. A woman frequently arrives at her conclusions by her intuition, which is based on her ability to perceive voice inflections and facial expressions. A man normally draws his conclusions through cold logic. By way of contrast, a family and a home constitute extensions of a woman, whereas a man's sense of identity normally comes from his job and his sporting activities. A woman's uppermost need is to be *cherished* by her husband. A man's most basic need is *admiration* for what he has accomplished in life. How much heartache in marriage could be avoided if only each partner could realize and accept these differences!

The Needed Core of Similarities

By way of summary, we can say that men and women differ from one another both physically and emotionally simply because they are males and females, and each must try to understand the opposite gender. They also differ in individual personality traits that cross the gender line. Each is drawn to the other by the personality that fulfills basic needs in his or her own emotional makeup. Lurking on the flip side of an individual's strengths, however, is a corresponding set of weaknesses. These must be understood and accepted if the marriage is to be a happy one.

While differences in the sexes and in personalities can be stimulating to a marriage if they are properly understood, harmony must be achieved in some very vital areas if lasting love and friendship is to be the result.

First, the most important area of agreement should be the couple's religious values. Differences in beliefs can be a constant source of irritation throughout marriage if each has strong convictions.

Second, husbands and wives should agree in their moral values. A person with a strong sense of what is morally right and wrong can never respect nor enjoy a close relationship with someone who lies, steals and breaks commitments.

Third, marriage partners should share an outlook on life that involves common goals, objectives, and a purpose for living. Simply stated, Where are you going in life? What do you hope to accomplish? Without an agreement in this crucial area, most couples are doomed to an existence of disagreement.

Fourth, husbands and wives who are truly one another's best friends should have many areas of mutual interests because this characteristic is vital for any type of lasting relationship. Friendships are drawn from the circle of those with whom we share activities and interests. Friends simply enjoy doing things together. Couples should enjoy enough individual differences to make life stimulating while also being bonded together by similar interests. How sad it is when husbands and wives suddenly find themselves living with total strangers as the children leave home because the only thing they had in common through the years was their offspring. Each of us should invite our mate to enter our world of interests, and we should take the initiative in becoming more interested in the pleasures of our partners.

Suggestions for Deep Friendships in Marriage

In far too many marriages, the partners simply endure each other. Faithful to their vows, many husbands and wives live parallel lives while sharing little in common. They certainly never achieve the status of being one another's best friend.

True friendship in marriage has its own special qualities. We are drawn to other people as friends because of personalities and common interests. Though some of those relationships last for a lifetime, they never have the exposure of a 24-hour-a-day marriage relationship. Husbands and wives see one another at their best and at their worst. As the years pass, each may tend to take the other for granted, and common courtesies — extended even to strangers — are frequently neglected. A marriage friendship requires special nurturing.

This chapter is being written in a very special place. For our 41st wedding anniversary, Don and I decided to revisit the site of our honeymoon. We managed to get reservations at the same hotel in a room just two doors down from the original one. The balcony still overlooks the ocean as it laps against the rocks beneath us, and the view is breathtaking. The setting has brought back a flood of memories as we have relived those first few days of our new life together. (We have even listened to the recording of our wedding.) In the beginning we thought we loved one another as much as we possibly could. The years have expanded our capacity for love, however, and the affection of those first days seems pale in comparison to the deep and abiding love we now share.

As the waves have rolled in and out, we have talked about all the water that has flowed under the bridge of our life together: our work together in the Lord's kingdom, the children, our travels, all the joys and sorrows we have shared. Each milestone has been very precious. Through all of it, we have seen God's providential hand.

Books, sermons and marriage seminars all give instructions for a happy marriage, but often the most lasting rules are learned by living. Through our 41 years together, the following simple bits of wisdom seem to have risen to the top. Perhaps they can be of help to you and to others who are seeking ways to strengthen their marriages and experience true friendship with one another:

Marriage is a sacred commitment. Amid all the splendor and details of a wedding, sometimes we forget the seriousness of those vows. Before God and witnesses, we are promising to live together until we are parted by death. Absolute sexual faithfulness is demanded by God. Unfaithfulness is the only reason for which the marriage can be dissolved while both parties are alive (Matthew 19:1-9).

Along with our commitment to the marriage vows should be the realization that we must learn to work out our differences because differences will exist. Almost any marriage could easily end in divorce at one time or another if the partners are guided solely by feelings. A willingness to learn coping skills is implied with every "I do." Marriage friendship is the only type of friendship that is sealed by a covenant. Others may come and go as the interest wanes.

God should be the third person in the marriage partnership.
It is only when a man and woman together bow in submission to
God's will that the marriage truly can be a happy one. When my husband and I were dating, the phrase "the three of us" emerged early
as we planned for our future. One's love for, and desire to serve, God
should be even greater than the love for one's spouse (Matthew 22:36-
40). Many problems never even surface when this proper spiritual
foundation has been laid.

Never take love for granted. Although the dating days are over
and a lifetime contract has been made, both the husband and the wife
should constantly continue to pursue the affection of the other. Only
then can there be lifetime happiness.

Remember common courtesies. How sad it is when we treat
complete strangers with greater politeness than we extend to our
mates. Simple words such as "please" and "thank you for doing that
for me" should be second nature to husbands and wives in dealing
with one another. And remember, so often it is the *tone* of the voice
that irritates rather than the actual words.

Remember that hurtful words leave lasting scars. In the heat
of a disagreement, we may say things that seem to relieve our own
frustrations at the moment, and later we can sincerely say we are
sorry and can be forgiven by God and our mate. But although the
arrow can be pulled out, the scar always remains in the heart of
the one who received the verbal blow. How much better it is to choose
our words wisely and never allow negative ones to cross our lips!

Problems should never be allowed to fester. Often an angry out-
burst is the result of accumulated layers of resentment over petty annoyances that have never been resolved. The last grievance was not
really that bad; it was just the proverbial straw that broke the camel's
back when it was tossed upon the heap of emotional garbage caused
by rotting resentments that had never been cleansed.

**Honest communication is essential in any close friendship, but
especially within the bonds of marriage.** We must be able to tell one
another when we are hurt or angry or frustrated if we are to resolve
problems before they multiply. However, no one is going to expose
true feelings if he or she is continually cut down and criticized. We

should be able to tell each other how we feel before the negative feelings have had time to inflame the relationship. This requires an atmosphere of love and trust that is slowly built, layer upon layer.

We probably will never completely understand the male-female differences in the marriage relationship. The physical differences are obvious. The emotional differences are far more obscure, but they exist. Most of what we need to learn can be learned simply by observing and listening to each other. The message is there; we just need to be perceptive enough to interpret it. Even if we can never understand the differences between men and women, at least we can *accept* them.

Husbands and wives also must accept the differences in individual personalities. As was mentioned earlier, no one can change the basic core of a person's personality. There is a vast difference in trying to help a person overcome a sin — for which he or she could be lost — and in striving to change a basic personality.

Try as we may, we are not going to make a neat person out of a messy one. The habitually late husband or wife probably never will arrive 10 minutes early, regardless of how much nagging we may do. A quiet, shy mate seldom will turn into the life of the party. Neither will a talkative person ever sit quietly by. Some people never will balance a checkbook.

Remember that the apostle Peter was always headstrong and impulsive. He sinned when he denied Christ, and he had to repent of this wrong (Matthew 26:69-75). Then the Master accepted the personality of this rugged fisherman as it was and channeled it into usefulness in His service. It was Peter's impetuousness that made him the perfect one to stand before the Jews on the Day of Pentecost and preach the first gospel sermon.

Acceptance is as necessary in the friendship of marriage as it is in any other type of friendship. Just remember that we all have our fair share of faults. If I want you to bear with my weaknesses until I can improve, then I must extend to you that same right.

Never belittle your mate, especially in the presence of others. We all have our weak points. If we want to make light of them, that is our privilege — but no one else has the right to ridicule us and poke fun at our shortcomings. If you want to help me overcome a fault, lovingly tell me in private. Never criticize, nor be sarcastic. Laugh with me but never at me. Remember that complimenting desired behavior is far more effective than criticizing the undesirable.

True friends allow space in their togetherness. Any friendship will suffer from possessiveness. None of us wants a friend who demands all our attention to the exclusion of anyone else. This is especially true within the boundaries of the marriage relationship.

Men tend to be activity oriented in their friendships. They enjoy the companionship of other men in doing things. They can play ball, fish, hunt or attend sporting events with their buddies for hours at a time and never touch upon their feelings. Most men don't even like to talk about their feelings. In fact, often they're not even sure how they feel.

Most women, on the other hand, equate friendship with talking about their feelings. Engaging in activities is secondary to sharing thoughts with one another.

A wife should be willing to allow her husband the freedom to do "guy things" with his buddies. She may never understand his passion for hunting, but then he probably never will fathom her enjoyment of shopping with another woman.

But we do not have to understand. We must merely accept the differences and allow freedom in our friendship with one another.

Make friendship with your mate a top priority in your life. Never take that friendship for granted because marital friendships require even more nurturing than other kinds because of the 24-hour exposure to one another.

Just how important is your marriage friendship? One way or the other, we usually find time to do whatever is really important to us. If we say we don't have time to spend with our mates, we really do not assign that relationship a top priority.

Friendships require time and effort. They don't just happen instantaneously, nor do they automatically endure.

Children demand time and can even be a strain on the relationship between husband and wife. Just remember that the best gift parents can give their children is their love for one another. That priority never should be forgotten.

Just how much time have you spent with your spouse during this past year? If you find that you no longer share common interests, the chances are good that you do not find delight in doing things together anymore.

How many activities have you done together recently — just the two of you? Do you ever have dinner out alone? How about an occasional getaway without friends or children? Friendship needs the proper soil for cultivation. All too often, marriage partners wake up one morning to find they are living with a complete stranger. The relationship has broken down because it was not nurtured.

After all, a friend is someone we enjoy being with and whose absence makes us feel lonely. The quality time spent with our mates should be a top priority.

Conclusion

Friendship should be the foundation of a marriage. A friend is someone we enjoy being with and with whom we share many interests and activities. It is someone with whom we can laugh as well as cry. It is a person we trust and in whom we can confide. A friend is someone whose achievements bring us pleasure and for whom we are willing to sacrifice. It is someone with whom we can relax and be ourselves.

Sexual affection may be the initial drawing card, but the marriage is doomed for failure unless a bedrock foundation of friendship develops through the years. Physical attraction wanes with the passing of time. Bodies have a tendency to become flabby. Wrinkles inevitably creep across once-flawless faces. Hair either turns gray or turns loose. The words "I want to spend my life with you" imply a lifetime of companionship — a friendship far deeper than those found in any other sort of friendship.

We all want to feel that we are special to someone as long as we both shall live. We want to feel that we can trust that person with our most intimate thoughts and know we never will be ridiculed or betrayed. We want to be accepted as we are. How wonderful it is when our lifetime partner is also our best friend!

Questions

1. Probably no other friendship exists with 24-hour-a-day exposure as does the relationship shared in marriage. Discuss the benefits as well as the problems inherent when two people live under the same roof.

2. Discuss the establishment of the first home according to the Genesis account. Why was it not good for Adam to be alone? In what ways was Eve a suitable companion? What went wrong during the early days of their marriage?

3. While dating, a young man and woman have limited exposure to one another and normally see only the strengths of the other. How can our mate's strengths offset our weaknesses? How can they draw us to each other? Is this good or bad?

4. In what sense do we marry the child locked inside our mates as well as the older person who is yet to develop? How can this reality affect the marriage relationship?

5. What determines our basic temperaments? Can the core ever be significantly changed?

6. Why are we normally attracted to someone whose basic temperament differs from our own? What are the advantages as well as the disadvantages?

7. What are the physical differences in men and women? In what ways do we also differ emotionally? How can this present problems in the marriage?

8. Discuss the necessity of agreement in the following areas if there is to be happiness in marriage: religious values, morals, outlook on life, and common interests.

9. Discuss the seriousness of the marriage vows. For what two reasons can a covenant be broken? How does this fact make it imperative that marriage partners learn to solve problems?

10. Why must our love for God be even greater than our love for one another in marriage (Matthew 22:36-40)?

11. Husbands and wives never should take their love for granted. What are some ways in which the courtship can continue throughout marriage?

12. Although hurtful words can be forgiven, they inevitably leave scars upon the heart. Yet, sometimes expressing deep feelings can be therapeutic. What is the solution to this challenge?

13. Unresolved resentment can be devastating. How can problems be nipped in the bud? Should marriage partners discuss everything that irritates them?

14. How does honest communication require love and trust? How do we learn to communicate?

15. Little can be done to change the basic core of someone's personality. How did God use rugged, impulsive Peter in the early days of the church?

16. Why should we never belittle our mates? How can we help them overcome a fault?

17. What are the advantages of allowing "space" in the togetherness of marriage?

18. Discuss the practicality of making friendship in marriage a priority.

19. Most of the principles in this chapter can be summarized in the words of Luke 6:31. Read this verse and discuss its application to marriage.

20. Discuss these verses, and apply them to the lesson: Proverbs 21:19; 25:24; 27:15.

CHAPTER 8

HANDLE WITH CARE

Friendships Within the Family

It has been said that we can choose our friends, but we have to take what we get when it comes to relatives. How true! While many of them become some of our dearest friends, sometimes relationships within the family become strained or even shattered. Most of the time we can walk away from an ordinary friendship if conditions become unbearable, but we are often locked into family units for the remainder of our lives. We are wise to foresee the potentiality of problems with relatives and take proper preventive measures before relationships become hostile.

Relationships with Our Children

A baby is totally dependent upon his parents for survival. Then for the next 18 years, we feed our children, walk the floor with them at night, sit by their bedsides, take them to the doctor, get them off to school, oversee their studies, cheer for them at ball games, and watch them become young adults. During all these years we do our best to instill in them the moral and religious principles that should form the foundation for their lives and develop the roots that will sustain them through the storms of life.

Imagine a child's life as a stream of water. At the bottom of the stream is a rockbed foundation of love. Even a baby senses the love of his parents and others in his little world, as well as the love of

God. Until children have first received love themselves, it is extremely difficult for them to give it. This love enables them to develop a sense of their own worth.

The banks of the stream are just as important as the rockbed foundation. These banks, which keep the child in the right channel, represent the discipline from loving parents as they set boundaries and enforce them.

During the teenage years, the child encounters many threatening crags in the stream of life. It is only normal for young people to question the moral principles we have tried to instill in them. God has no grandchildren. Those of each generation must search the Scriptures for themselves and personally accept those principles, not simply because their parents have taught them that a matter is right or wrong, but because they have searched the Scriptures themselves and have formed their own convictions.

Another crag is the inherent danger of peer pressure as the child so desperately tries to be like everyone around him. The crag of identity appears, too, as the teenager seeks to determine who he is and discover his place in the world. The rocks of sex and drug problems also loom as threats during the adolescent years.

During the first quarter of our children's lives, an equality in the parent-child relationship should not exist. Parents should be the authority figures as they lovingly guide their offspring around the crags of childhood into the mainstream of the adult world.

Little by little our children are taught independence until they have developed wings strong enough for flying. It has wisely been observed that the two most priceless possessions we can give our children are roots and wings. May we never forget that the wings are just as important as the roots.

At this stage we cease being the authority figures in our children's lives as they leave our sheltering arms of parenthood. Whether or not they return to us as adult friends may very well depend upon how successful we've been in giving them roots and wings during their first 18 years.

After the Wedding

Weddings are milestones in our lives because they seem to signal an entry into the adult world even more than our leaving home to pursue a career. When the wedding is over and all the guests and members of the wedding party have departed, the parents of both the bride and groom are left with a mixture of feelings. How close will the young couple be to their parents from now on? How will the members of the extended family get along with one another?

A new commitment has been sealed. The loyalty once given to the parents now shifts to the new spouse because a separation has been made: "Therefore shall a man leave his father and his mother, and shall cleave unto his wife: and they shall be one flesh" (Genesis 2:24). Leaving is not deserting but is the establishing of a new loyalty that is stronger than the first. The period of time after the wedding is one of adjustment as everyone involved works to strengthen in-law relationships.

The backgrounds of the two extended families may sometimes be similar, but usually they are miles apart. The members of one family may place a great emphasis on neatness while the others may not. One may have strong holiday traditions while the other family's observances may be very casual and unimportant. The bride may have grown up in an atmosphere of expressive affection while the groom may have lived in a world where few feelings were expressed. If the marriage is to succeed, many compromises must be made.

Not only must each set of parents accept the fact that they have said goodbye to the child they've nurtured for so many years, but they also have said hello to a new family member. Until recently, this person had been a stranger to them. Now he has become part of the extended family unit. Adjustments undoubtedly will have to be made.

Many jokes have been made concerning mothers-in-law. Most of the conflict seems to be centered between the bride and mother of the groom who, typically, has been the primary care giver of her son all his life. Marriage marks the passing of the torch to the bride, and some mothers are reluctant. A new wife may feel she is in competition with her husband's mother in the realm of cooking and running the house. The problem often is compounded when the groom unfavorably compares his wife's culinary and housekeeping skills to those of his mother.

Cutting the Apron Strings

As parents we have been entrusted with the task of guiding a totally helpless infant through all the stages of childhood while assisting him in gaining the necessary traits to live independently in the adult world. The whole process can be impeded by these hindrances:

Some parents do too much for their children. They usually mean well, but their actions harm their children's ability to function as adults. A parent who refuses to cut the apron strings is being unfair to the child. Gradually, young people must be allowed to use their own judgments as they mature, but they also must be permitted to accept the consequences of their mistakes. Parents of adult children no longer control them. They cannot expect their offspring to call or write as frequently as the parents might like. Neither can they make their decisions for them.

While some parents do too much for their children, others give them too much. Instead of instant gratification, we all need to learn to wait for what we want. We seldom appreciate things that are handed to us on a silver platter. Instant gratification only leads to selfishness, which is a leading factor in the breakup of many marriages.

Other parents set few guidelines for behavior during the early years. Their children, who usually run wild, are a terror to everyone. As they become adults and enter into marriage, they are poor risks in this new relationship.

The success of a marriage depends largely upon how well the bride and groom have been successful in becoming independent adults before they enter into the marriage covenant.

As our own children were leaving the shelter of our home and entering the transitory world of the college campus, one morning I sat on our front porch and wrote the following words:

In Psalm 127 children are compared to arrows — arrows that are shot into the future by their parents. At the time of aiming, most mothers and fathers could utter these words to their offspring:

> It could not possibly have been 18 years since you were first placed into our arms. During the time of diapers, middle-of-the-night feedings, and days of being tied down with a little child, your leaving seemed so remote. How quickly those years have flown by! As parents we have made mistakes because we are only human. Please forgive our blunders. For years we have tried to instill God's principles into your hearts because we've known your eternal destiny is dependent upon following His Word. The time has come for you to test those principles and to accept them as your own. You are now an independent adult, and we are so very proud of you. Always remember that, although you will be leaving us physically, you never can leave our love and concern because they will go with you to the four corners of the earth. As the arrow is shot forth, we will always be at home watching and praying that the winds of life will not blow you off the course we have set you upon. Goodbye, my child.

Scriptural Advice

Some basic principles of Christian living — loving one another, being kind and tenderhearted — are the basis for good in-law relationships. All family members would do well to heed the admonitions contained in these scriptures:

1. "Blessed are the peacemakers: for they shall be called the children of God" (Matthew 5:9).

2. "If it be possible, as much as lieth in you, live peaceably with all men" (Romans 12:18).

3. "I therefore, the prisoner of the Lord, beseech you that ye walk worthy of the vocation wherewith ye are called, With all lowliness and meekness, with long-suffering, forebearing one another in love" (Ephesians 4:1-2).

4. "Let all bitterness, and wrath, and anger, and clamor, and evil speaking, be put away from you, with all malice: And be ye kind one to another, tender-hearted, forgiving one another, even as God for Christ's sake hath forgiven you" (Ephesians 4:31-32).

5. "Follow peace with all men" (Hebrews 12:14).

The Bible gives us several instances of both good and bad in-law relationships. Probably the most well-known story is that of Ruth and Naomi, which is considered in depth in another chapter of this study. The relationship between these two in-laws was so strong that Ruth was willing to leave her own family and her familiar culture to follow Naomi to a strange land, a different culture, and even another religion.

The story of Moses and Jethro, his father-in-law, is another example of good in-law relationships. As leader of the Israelites, Moses had heavy responsibilities, but he began to grow weary under the load of leading the people while also settling their disagreements. Jethro questioned Moses' wisdom in judging the people and told him plainly:

"The thing that thou doest is not good. Thou wilt surely wear away, both thou, and this people that is with thee: for ... thou art not able to perform it thyself alone" (Exodus 18:17-18).

Jethro then advised his son-in-law to select godly men to judge the people so Moses could concentrate upon leadership:

"So Moses hearkened to the voice of his father in law, and did all that he had said. And Moses chose able men out of all Israel, and made them heads over the people, rulers of thousands, rulers of hundreds, rulers of fifties, and rulers of tens. And they judged the people at all seasons: the hard causes they brought unto Moses, but every small matter they judged themselves. And Moses let his father-in-law depart; and he went his way into his own land" (Exodus 18:24-27).

The Bible also shares examples of negative in-law relationships. Esau, the son of Isaac and Rebekah, chose two Hittite wives, Judith and Bashemath. Genesis 26:35 reveals that the women "were a grief of mind unto Isaac and to Rebekah." After Jacob had angered his brother by using trickery to obtain the birthright, Esau hated Jacob and even wanted to kill him. Rebekah intervened, urging her younger son to flee to her own homeland for his own safety as well as to select a wife. Her frustration was voiced in these words:

> "I am weary of my life because of the daughters of Heth: if Jacob take a wife of the daughters of Heth, such as these which are of the daughters of the land, what good shall my life do me?" (Genesis 27:46).

Another example of a poor in-law relationship is that of Saul and David. The lives of King Saul and the young boy David had been intertwined for a number of years as David matured from a humble shepherd boy to a hero of the people. David married Michal, the daughter of King Saul, but Saul became extremely jealous of the young man whom he considered to be his rival for the throne. Saul's actions became particularly obnoxious when he unsuccessfully tried to have his son-in-law killed in his own bed (1 Samuel 19:11-17). The disagreements of Saul and David are chronicled over a period of approximately 10 years as the king relentlessly sought the fugitive: "for the king of Israel is come out to seek a flea, as when one doth hunt a partridge in the mountains" (1 Samuel 26:20).

Practical Suggestions for In-law Relationships

New in-law relationships should be approached with optimism. Regardless of the stories we have heard, an in-law is not always a curse. Indeed, many prove to be loving, lifetime friends. Much depends upon laying a positive foundation. These relationships cannot be rushed but should be allowed to unfold with the passing of time. It is wise, therefore, not to be too aggressive in the beginning. Accept one another with friendly, open arms and allow time to tell how deep the relationship eventually will become.

Following these suggestions could be the first step toward a long, successful relationship with your child and his or her new mate:

Do not meddle in the lives of your adult children. Advice should be given very sparingly. Having offered them unsolicited advice since early childhood, this is sometimes difficult to do. But it is now best to wait until asked for your opinions, unless the situation involves a wrong that could affect their eternal destiny.

Parents should remember that their children are now adults. Let them make their own decisions as well as their own mistakes.

Parents should not expect to be included in their children's social lives. It is wise to back off, give them some privacy, and wait for an invitation. The more diversified the interests of the parents are, the greater the chances they will let go gracefully. Those who have had few activities outside of the rearing of their children often find it difficult to function as independent adults themselves. When the children leave home, it is time for parents to get on with their own lives. They now have new roles to fill and will be happiest when they can assume them cheerfully.

Parents should beware of criticism. The young couple undoubtedly will do many things differently than you might, and we may not appreciate their choices — of furniture, houses, cars or even careers. Because we can accept the uniqueness of friends outside the family relationship, we should give our own children the same freedom to be themselves.

Allow the bride and groom to develop their own family traditions. Both bring to the marriage the customs of their own childhoods. Just because one family always celebrated the Christmas holidays, Thanksgiving or birthdays in a certain manner, there is no valid reason for a new home to continue handling those special times in the same way unless it chooses to do so. Many family arguments have erupted over whether the newlyweds will eat Christmas dinner with her family or his. Which family gets them for Christmas Eve festivities? When distance is a factor, will there be alternate holidays spent at the home of each set of parents? In the midst of all the inherent bickering, one wonders what sort of traditions the new home is being allowed to establish for itself.

Many other similar problems face parents and their adult children. The solution is for everyone to be understanding of each other's feelings while reaching some reasonable compromises.

Parents are not the only ones who need some pointers in making the transition during this time of life. The adult children bear an equal part of the responsibility in making the change a smooth one. Keeping these thoughts in mind can help ease the process:

Try to step into the shoes of both sets of parents, and imagine their feelings. We may resent interference from our parents, but until we've had our own children, we have no idea just how much love and concern are involved in rearing a child. We may say they are meddling in our lives, but a marriage ceremony never can sever the love parents feel for their own flesh and blood. This is the human being they have nurtured and for whom they have invested a major part of their adult lives. As a young married couple, we really cannot know how they feel until we stand with our own children at the threshold of their adult years.

Remember that your in-laws get much of the credit for nurturing the many wonderful qualities in your mate that first attracted you. Whether by genes or by rearing, we all bear the marks of our own parents. They leave their stamp on us for life. Rather than criticize our in-laws for their interference, we probably could turn the tide by listing all the special qualities that caused us to fall in love with their child and by thanking them for each characteristic they nurtured.

Realize that much of what we may call "interference" could very well be the parents' misguided desire to be of help. Rather than allowing resentment to build, the best course of action is usually frank discussion about the feelings of both sides, just as we would discuss grievances between ourselves and any other friends. We should listen to the advice offered by parents or in-laws and evaluate it. If it seems to be worthwhile, we would be wise to follow it. If it doesn't seem to be the best solution, we should thank them and do what we think is best.

Sometimes the shoe is on the other foot, and it is the adult children who offer advice to their parents and in-laws. Remember that the parents should have equal rights in accepting or rejecting that advice. The same spirit of independence that prompts the young adult to rebel against parental interference also manifests itself in the rebellion of the older person who wants her children to quit telling her what to do.

Undoubtedly, disagreements will arise between husband and wife — and those differences can be resolved much more quickly if the couple's dirty linen is not aired before other family members. If the adult children run home each time there is friction, parents usually will take sides, often creating barriers that may remain between the couple and the parents and in-laws long after the conflict has been settled between husband and wife. Such obstacles never should be allowed to develop. (Incidentally, some physical distance between both sets of parents and their children is recommended. Neither family needs to know everything that happens in the lives of the other side.)

Members of physical families are wise to follow the instructions given for handling disagreements between two members of God's spiritual family. Matthew 18:15-17 instructs us first to go directly to the person with whom we have a disagreement and try to resolve the problem without telling other spiritual family members. Only when dialogue between the two individuals fails should others be brought into the dispute. The same general guidelines are advisable within a physical family.

We should realize that strong ties naturally exist between children and their parents. Allegiance to the new union may require some time and understanding. Each family has its own peculiarities, which may be irritating at times. When expressing our feelings to our mates, we should understand their natural defensiveness.

Because our parents and in-laws inevitably will try to tell us what to do at times, we are wise to learn to accept criticism gracefully. We should listen to such criticism objectively, as a germ of truth often is hidden beneath the sometimes harsh outer layers: "He that answereth a matter before he heareth it, it is folly and shame unto him" (Proverbs 18:13).

Other passages from Proverbs reinforce this principle: "Poverty and shame shall be to him that refuseth instruction: but he that regardeth reproof shall be honored" (13:18); "Apply thine heart unto instruction, and thine ears to the words of knowledge" (23:12); and "As an earring of gold, and an ornament of fine gold, so is a wise reprover upon an obedient ear" (25:12).

The Answer

Love is the lubricant that enables most family relationships to function smoothly as they work their way through the necessary adjustments of living in close emotional proximity.

Parents understandably desire love and respect from their grown children, but they no longer have the right to expect obedience as they once did. Love, on the part of everyone involved, cannot be demanded; it is a gift that must be given freely. With proper nurturance, all can come together in a mature, adult-to-adult relationship.

We must remember that family relationships, more than any other kind, need constant lubrication if major problems are to be avoided. We never want in-laws to become out-laws!

Questions

1. How do relationships within the family differ from other friendships?
2. Discuss the analogy of a child's life and a stream of water. What is the rockbed foundation? What do the banks represent? What is the significance of the crags?
3. Discuss the advice, "Wise parents voluntarily close the door to their children's adult lives on the outside before it is slammed from the inside." What does this mean, and do you agree or disagree?
4. What are the two most priceless possessions we can give our children?
5. When children enter the adult world, their parents cease to be the authority figures in their lives. Whether or not they return to their parents as adult friends depends on what two things?
6. At the time of the wedding vows, according to Genesis 2:24, where should new allegiances be placed?
7. How may the backgrounds of the newlyweds' extended families differ? What problems could arise as a result of these differences?
8. Why may the bride and her mother-in-law have particular problems in adjusting?

9. The lesson mentioned three hindrances to cutting the apron strings. Discuss these and add to the list.

10. Psalm 127:4 compares children to arrows. What is the purpose of an arrow?

11. Discuss the implications of these verses as they apply to family relationships: Matthew 5:9; Romans 12:18; Ephesians 4:1-2, 31-32; and Hebrews 12:14.

12. Discuss the biblical accounts of these in-law relationships: Ruth and Naomi; Moses and Jethro; Rebekah and the wives of Esau; and Saul and David.

13. In the lesson, parents were given four practical suggestions for in-law relationships. Discuss each one and add to the list.

14. The bride and groom also have responsibilities in creating harmonious in-law relationships. Discuss the six mentioned, particularly noting the advice from Proverbs, and expand the list with your own suggestions.

15. Love is the lubricant that enables families to adjust. Can love be demanded? What is the solution?

CHAPTER 9

HANDLE WITH CARE

Friendships During the Golden Years

During each phase of life, our friendships present their own unique set of benefits, as well as their own problems. But perhaps no other time of life brings as many rewards and challenges as the golden years.

As children and teenagers we were constantly busy with school activities. Our friends would come and go, depending upon which club we happened to select or which ball team chose us. Friendships were not a particular problem. If we made a move or changed activities, old friends faded into the background as newer ones came into focus.

As time passed, school friends were generally replaced by the companionship of young singles and then by the relationships of other married couples. We were caught up in a whirlwind of job changes, new locations, and settling in different communities while also trying to keep up with our own children and their varied interests. Life was characterized by hurrying, creating, investigating possibilities, making decisions, and extending ourselves to experience as much of life as possible. Old friends frequently were replaced by new ones as a matter of course, and life went on as normal. In fact, friends often were taken for granted; seldom was any serious thought given to the significance of lasting relationships. Paramount in our minds was the ambition to make our mark in the world.

But one day we realize the last child has left home and we're no longer involved in dashing frantically from one event to another. Our homes have ceased to be centers for children's activities as we've settled into a different phase of our lives: the middle years.

At this stage, many of us are still in relatively good health and enjoy most of the activities of our younger years, though perhaps at a slower pace, while we continue working at our jobs. Sometimes aging parents require our extra attention, but generally we enjoy more opportunities to dine out with other couples, deepen friendships, and engage in activities for which we had little time in earlier years.

The Wisdom of the Middle Years

Often during this time of life, we women pause to ponder the significance of relationships. While youth tends to take friends for granted, maturity realizes and treasures the worth of true friendships. This is a time of reflection, of sorting out what is meaningful and what is trivial. By now we have experienced much of the good and some of the bad that life has to offer, and we reflect upon all the friends who have crossed our paths. Many of the flames of youthful friendships have faded into faint memories, but a chosen few have found places in our hearts and will always be there as glowing embers. Though distance may separate us, and though there may be long periods of silence between us, we always seem to feel especially close to them. The dropping of a note in the mailbox or the dialing of the telephone enables us to resume our relationships immediately with these true friends.

The middle years, generally considered to be the ages of 45 to 65, can be extremely busy, but they do tend to provide us with more time to distinguish between the urgent and the truly important demands upon us. When the children were at home, the urgent clamored for most of our waking hours, and many of our friendships were shallow as we related to so many people. Little time was left to invest in deep relationships outside our immediate families.

By the time of our middle years, most of us have become aware that our bodies are slowing down, and we may have lost some of the urgency for getting things done. With the passing of years, however, comes wisdom. We now realize how much our deepest friendships have meant to us, and we evaluate our own mistakes in relating to others and try to correct them. We also realize how empty life would be without friends during the winter months that lie ahead.

By now we have learned — often through trial and error — some important principles of relating to others. We have more time to do important things with our friends and to linger over a cup of coffee rather than dashing off to the next activity. It is a period of strengthening old friendships and making new ones. We have become aware that relationships require care and cultivation, and we finally realize that friends are far more important than "things." How sad that many of us take so long to discover that nugget of gold!

We now also know how important it is to be accepted as we are, warts and all. During these years the friends who mean the most to us are those who wrap their loving arms of acceptance around us. In turn, we are able to extend our own unconditional love to others as friendships assume a far deeper meaning.

Winter-Spring Relationships

Although we do tend to gravitate toward those within our own age group, the golden years of life provide excellent opportunities for friendships between older and younger generations.

Paul, realizing the valuable knowledge of mature women, told Titus to instruct the older women to set an example for the younger women by the way they lived. In addition to being good patterns, the experienced women were to teach the younger ones how to live godly lives and how to be good wives and mothers:

> "The aged women likewise, that they be in behavior as becometh holiness, not false accusers, not given to much wine, teachers of good things; That they may teach the young women to be sober, to love their husbands, to love their children, To be discreet, chaste, keepers at home, good, obedient to their own husbands, that the word of God be not blasphemed" (Titus 2:3-5).

While it is true that older women may have gray hair, more wrinkles, and thicker waistlines than their young counterparts, most of them realize what is important in life. Younger women can profit from the experience of the mature woman, who already has walked the path of life and has learned to avoid the rocks that can impede their progress.

The older woman, however, must be careful not to instruct the younger until asked. Such a practice borders on meddling and can only cause trouble. Mature women first should gain the confidence of the younger women by the manner in which they live (Titus 2:3). Once this respect is earned, and the lines of communication are open, the younger generation should take the next step.

Elizabeth and Mary provide an excellent example of a winter-spring relationship. The depth of feelings experienced by Mary, a teenage Jewish girl, when told she would shortly give birth to the promised Messiah, is difficult for us to fathom. Dare we try to imagine her shame under the wagging tongues of the town? Scripture tells us that Mary "went into the hill country with haste" (Luke 1:39) to stay with her much older relative, Elizabeth, who was approximately six months pregnant at the time.

For the next three months, young Mary lived with her aged cousin and husband in a strange town, away from other relatives, childhood friends, and the man to whom she was engaged to be married. She must have had many questions for Elizabeth. How wonderful it must have been to spend three months with an older woman who respected and loved her own husband! Mary undoubtedly learned many lessons from her cousin.

We may conclude that the successful winter-spring relationship is usually based on casual encounters between an older person and a younger friend who admires and respects the life of the older one and who seeks informal opportunities to profit from her wisdom. In turn, the older person should be open to the younger one and should be honest about her own humanity. No one is drawn to someone who believes she herself never makes mistakes.

While a mentoring friendship is normally evaluated in terms of the benefits realized by the younger woman, the story of Ruth and

Naomi illustrates the value of the relationship to the older woman. Ruth certainly profited from the advice and example of her mother-in-law, but Naomi reaped many benefits, too. Because Ruth and Boaz cared for her, she had security in her old age. She also received love and respect when little Obed was entrusted to her care. Both Ruth and Naomi were winners in the relationship.

Scripture gives us other examples of winter-spring relationships. Consider Abraham and Isaac as well as Paul and his young friends, Timothy and John Mark.

Hindrances to Friendship During the Golden Years

While many wonderful advantages are born of friendships during the golden years, the latter part of this phase of life can also have its problems. These years may present conditions not encountered before. Consider these situations:

Loneliness. The latter years of life often rob us of the companionship of a lifelong mate as death takes its inevitable toll. We may become enveloped in an indescribable loneliness as we no longer fit into the lives of others in the same manner. Instead of being a comfortable half of a pair, we find ourselves a lonely half that is no longer part of a whole.

Physical Abilities. As we get older, more parts of our bodies fail to function as they should. Often we experience more discomfort than we've ever encountered before, joints do not bend as they once did, and it is more difficult to move around. Physical weakness can make it a struggle just to get through the day.

"Cast me not off in the time of old age; forsake me not when my strength faileth" (Psalm 71:9).

Declining Health. Declining health can have harmful effects upon friendships. Staying at home becomes easier than exerting the effort to mingle among other people. Having others into our homes becomes more difficult, and withdrawal into our own little nests of comfort can become a habit. After a while, we sometimes quit trying.

Financial Restrictions. A lack of money can become a problem during retirement years on a fixed income. When funds are scarce, inviting a friend to go out for lunch or shopping is more difficult. Tight finances can limit the amount of money we believe we can spare for long-distance telephone calls or cards to stay in touch. Entertaining in our homes can be expensive, too.

Freedom of Movement. The lack of transportation can prevent our circulation among friends. Age or other health problems can limit our freedom to come and go as we please.

New Surroundings. Sometimes moving to another place to be near a child or other care giver seems to be the sensible course of action. Whenever we pull up roots, however, we usually leave little pieces of our hearts behind. A new neighborhood is never quite the same as the old one, and because we do not circulate as freely as we once did, we do not usually make friends as readily as before. People in the new neighborhood or new church home have their own circles of friends, and we may feel left out.

Death of Friends. As we advance in age, it is only natural for death to claim more and more of our longtime friends. It becomes easier to sit at home than to exert the energy to get out and make new friends.

Attitude. Age has a tendency to stymie the acceptance of inevitable change. While some changes are not good, others improve conditions. Older people frequently become set in their ways and resent changes without first evaluating the possible outcomes. Such attitudes can shut people out of our lives.

Personality Traits. Advancing age frequently intensifies our normal traits of character. There is a connection between the end and the beginning of life. Loving and caring elderly people were, for the most part, loving and caring as younger people. We are molded by lifetime attitudes and are composites of every thought we have had, every word we have spoken, and every deed we have done. Our friends may tolerate a certain amount of unpleasantness when we are younger, but when bad traits become more glaring as we age, many people may find us so disagreeable that they simply leave us alone.

Self-Centeredness. As our own problems intensify with age, it becomes easy to dominate conversations with a recital of our own woes. Often we fail to show an interest in the problems of others as well as ways that we can help them. A self-centered person is not appealing to most of us.

Cynicism. We are wise if we face the fact that life is not always fair. We sometimes get the bad breaks when we do not deserve them. Many times unworthy people seem to have all the good luck. During earlier times we tend to shrug off injustice and get on with our lives. During the last years we sometimes become cynical and build impenetrable walls that shut others out.

Making the Golden Years the Best Ones

Contentment during the last part of our lives is more directly related to what is happening within us than what is happening to us. Although we have little control over our external circumstances, with the help of God we can have mastery over ourselves. The right attitude is the key to meaningful golden years:

Be willing to let go of youth. By this time of life, most of us have become aware that we no longer can do things in the same manner as we did when we were younger. Stamina diminishes as our physical bodies require more time to perform the same tasks. Though we may slow down, in so doing we are able to notice many everyday moments we previously took for granted.

We also realize that our appearance has changed. How sad it is to see an older person who insists upon trying to act and look like a teenager! Not only is the effort impossible, but it ignores the beauty of maturity. Youth may have the freshness of spring, but maturity has the breathtaking colors of autumn. Let us not fail to nurture the glorious hues of our own fall foliage simply because we refuse to give up the green crispness of spring. After all, how many people drive to New England to see the spring leaves?

We would do well to incorporate the wisdom of Paul into our lives when we take to heart his words:

"This one thing I do, forgetting those things which are behind, and reaching forth unto those things which are before, I press toward the mark for the prize of the high calling of God in Christ Jesus" (Philippians 3:13-14).

Invest time and effort in keeping our bodies functioning at their fullest potential. Naturally, the aging process affects all of us physically, but keeping all parts oiled and running at maximum possible strength is very important. Good nutrition, exercise, and proper preventive medical supervision can work wonders in helping our physical bodies function as they should. Remember that they are temples of God and should be treated with respect (1 Corinthians 3:16-17). A healthy body can better relate to others than one that is preoccupied in dealing with the discomforts of aging. When others ask, "How are you?" they really do not want an organ recital. Only a doctor should be given a complete answer to such a question.

Use the mind or lose it. The parable of the talents in Matthew 25:14-30 teaches that we should use, to the fullest, whatever ability God has given us. The mind is like any other body part; it must be used or it will atrophy. Until the 1960s the general consensus of opinion was that most elderly people slip in their memory and problem-solving skills, and begin to think slowly and illogically. More recent studies have proven that theory to be false. Barring such misfortunes as Alzheimer's disease, many older brains either improve with age or maintain a high level of mental functioning. A smaller number of older brains do decrease in ability because of health problems — not because of age — but most of those are failing simply because they are not used regularly.

As we become older, we are generally less active and may fall into a passive lifestyle conducive to a lack of use of our minds and bodies. The wise person, however, looks ahead down the road of the golden years and makes realistic plans for mental stimulation. She will continue reading about new things, expanding her knowledge. She may want to enroll in classes of some kind. Developing new skills is a challenge. One of my dear friends delighted me when she said she had begun taking violin lessons in her 80s.

Each day of our lives should be a challenge to increase our mental capacities. An alert mind can make new friendships and maintain old ones more easily than a brain that has deteriorated from disuse.

Be grateful. Early in life we should develop an attitude of expecting nothing from others, being grateful instead for any small kindnesses done for us. If we try to make friends and relatives feel guilty for not visiting or writing or for neglecting us in any other way, they are sure to have little desire to be with us. In fact, such an attitude usually drives them away. No one owes us anything. Our genuine gratitude for any favors can pave the path for additional kindnesses.

Plan outside activities. It is wise to plan activities that will get us out of the house and circulating among other people at least four or five times a week. Such a commitment can be the impetus to get us on our feet and going, even when we do not feel up to par.

Make at least one new friend each year. True, many dear friends have either passed away or moved to a new location, and the making of new friendships requires effort. All too often we become contented to sit at home and feel sorry for ourselves. "A man that hath friends must show himself friendly: and there is a friend that sticketh closer than a brother" (Proverbs 18:24).

Take the initiative in making the first move. A dear friend wrote me concerning the loneliness she felt when she moved to a new town to be near one of her children. She had tried to become involved but still felt like an outsider. Then she happened to notice an opportunity and took advantage of it. She began having a young couple from church, along with the unmarried youth minister, over for dinner each Wednesday evening before the church services. Home-cooked meals were a delight to the young man, who normally had to cook for himself, and to the young husband and his wife, who normally had to dash home from work to prepare the evening meal before the midweek service.

When we no longer have a mate and people may no longer include us in their invitations, rather than feel sorry for ourselves, we may plan a simple luncheon ourselves and ask several other widows over for a period of fellowship. Or we can sit in different places at the church building and introduce ourselves to those who are strangers to us as we step out and take the risk!

Look for opportunities to encourage and praise people of all ages. Paul lavished praise and recognition upon his fellow Christians. A perusal of Romans 16 reveals his custom of expressing approval to those who had done noteworthy work in the kingdom. The names may be a bit strange to our ears, but the message is clear as Paul used some of these words of acknowledgement: "a servant of the church, a helper of many"; "my fellow workers who risked their own necks for my life, to whom not only I give thanks, but also all the churches of the Gentiles"; "my beloved"; "who labored much for us"; "who are of note among the apostles"; "my beloved in the Lord"; "our fellow worker in Christ"; and "who have labored much in the Lord."

When someone does something commendable, we should tell him. Most of us would agree with Mark Twain when he said, "I can live for two months on one good compliment." Even better is putting our words of praise in writing so the recipient can read our message many times. Perhaps a young man finally summons enough courage to direct a song at worship services. Write him a note of appreciation and wish him many more years of usefulness in the Lord's service. We should look constantly for the commendable things that others do.

If someone is sick, has lost a loved one, or is facing some other difficult situation, drop her a note with a few words of encouragement. Nearly everyone enjoys being remembered on birthdays or anniversaries. Like Barnabas, we all should try to be encouragers.

Learn to be flexible and roll with the punches. Life involves changes, and sometimes those changes do not always seem fair. Often we do not like the discomfort of conditions that are different, but when we cannot do anything about it, we are happier — and so is everyone around us — if we refuse to be stubborn and set in our ways. Rigidity can cause us to snap, but flexibility can enable us to make it through many difficult situations.

Take one day at a time, and look for the good in it. Often the path that lies ahead seems long and difficult, but we can make it for just one day. And though each day has its precious moments, many times we overlook them because we are focused only on our negative thoughts. Long ago I began a journal of notes concerning everyday, though seldom noticed, events that have brought me much happiness. An unknown writer expressed this thought: "What are you saving in your memory bin as food for the restless soul when the winter of life comes?"

The winter of life will come to all of us if we live long enough. Our own memory bins can be filled with precious moments if only we choose to notice them along the path of each day's journey and capture them in some sort of permanent form for later remembrance. In fact, the practice of searching for everyday treasures should be a lifetime habit because there is always something good about each day. An attitude of looking for the good instead of the bad is helpful in developing a character that attracts others rather than repelling them.

> "This is the day which the Lord hath made; we will rejoice and be glad in it" (Psalm 118:24).

Have a purpose in life that is more important than any external circumstances. Of all the people in this world, Christians should have the most meaningful purpose for living. When we become absorbed in serving God throughout our lifetimes, we have a reason for living that is more important than any obstacle in our path.

Conclusion

With God's help, and with the application of so many biblical principles to our lives, the last years should be the best of all. This part of life normally exchanges the frantic rush of career advancement and all the many demands of a busy family for a different pace, which allows time to sort the trivial activities from the important ones.

Sometimes adverse circumstances, such as poor health or dwindling finances, can have a diminishing effect upon the latter years if we allow them to take charge of our lives. The key is attitude, but a good attitude is seldom developed during trying times. Instead, our characters are molded throughout a lifetime.

Sowing the seeds of friendship is an ongoing process. We do not selfishly try to scatter them just because we are older, lonely, and may need companionship. Instead, we sow them as long as we live because the practice is pleasing to God. Proper sowing, in addition to the weeding of our own negative thoughts, can produce a field of beautiful friendships throughout a lifetime, but most especially during the golden years. By that time we have finally discovered that such relationships are some of the most valuable assets in life.

Our needs during the latter years may very well parallel those of Paul in 2 Timothy 4:9-13. After he had been serving God for many years and was imprisoned, he asked Timothy to bring him some things he needed during this phase of his life.

1. Paul needed companionship. He told Timothy to come as soon as he could and to bring John Mark with him.

2. Timothy also was asked to bring Paul's cloak. Prison cells were damp, and Paul realized he should properly care for his own physical body.

3. The apostle requested "the books." Paul continued stretching his mind through reading.

4. He desired "especially the parchments." He wanted to have the Scriptures with him during this time. His spiritual nature needed nourishment during his last years as well as during the first ones.

5. Perhaps Paul's most compelling need was not found in the requests he made of Timothy, but in the foundation upon which they all rested. This apostle to the Gentiles continued to have a purpose in life, a thrust that kept him on course. Simply stated, his life was dedicated to serving God. In Philippians 3:13-14 he used these words:

> "This one thing I do, forgetting those things which are behind, and reaching forth unto those things which are before, I press toward the mark for the prize of the high calling of God in Christ Jesus."

As a young man, when Paul learned that his lifetime direction was wrong, he abandoned his role as a Pharisee and rerouted his life to become Christianity's most influential spokesman. That purpose, that desire in his life, never abated but became even more powerful during his last days.

During the golden years, our needs are similar to those of Paul. We, too, need human companionship and proper care for our physical bodies, as well as nourishment for both the intellectual and spiritual parts of our beings. Most important, we must have a never-ending purpose in life. By keeping things in their proper perspective, we can have fulfilling years at the end of our lives if our own five basic needs are met.

Questions

1. Contrast the middle years with the preceding ones in relation to the pace of life and types of friendships one has.
2. What benefits do the middle years have to offer? What are some of the lessons we have learned by this time of life?
3. In Titus 2:3-5, what were the older women told to teach the younger ones? Why was their own behavior a prerequisite to their instruction?
4. Discuss the winter-spring relationship of Elizabeth and Mary. Why do you suppose Mary left Nazareth to live with a relative in a distant town? What could she have learned from Elizabeth?
5. The story of Ruth and Naomi is an excellent example of the friendship between two women — one older and one younger. Review the chapter relating to them, and make a list of the factors that made this relationship a success. How did Ruth profit? What were Naomi's benefits?
6. What do the examples of Abraham and Isaac, as well as Paul and his young friends Timothy and John Mark, teach us?
7. This lesson contains a list of 11 hindrances to friendships during the latter years of life. Assign them to teams of two for discussion and then report to the entire class. Do you feel that these hindrances are valid? Add to the list.
8. Do you agree with the statement that it is usually best to be willing to let go of youth? If so, in what ways do we do this? Incorporate a discussion of Paul's willingness to forget the past and concentrate on one major thrust in life.
9. How can a weakened body be a hindrance to the making and nurturing of friendships? What can we do to prevent or improve upon this condition?

10. Do aging minds automatically deteriorate? What can be done to keep them working to their fullest potential?
11. How can expecting favors from others damage relationships?
12. What are some activities that retired people can plan to do to get them out of the house and keep them circulating among other people? Why is this important?
13. Discuss the idea of making at least one new friend per year.
14. What does Proverbs 18:24 teach?
15. Why is it sometimes difficult to make the first move in making new friendships? Discuss some of the suggestions given in the lesson.
16. How can showing encouragement and praise open the door to new friendships? What are some practical suggestions for developing this habit?
17. Discuss Paul's praise of his friends in Romans 16.
18. How can flexibility in our nature be a factor in developing and nurturing friendships?
19. Why is it so important to look for the good in each day? What are some suggestions that will help us to develop this sort of attitude?
20. How can a purpose in life overcome any external circumstances?
21. Paul's requests to Timothy (2 Timothy 4:9-13) are similar to our needs during the golden years of our lives. Discuss the four requests as well as the foundation upon which they all rested.
22. Why should sowing the seeds of friendship be a practice that extends for a lifetime? What should be our reason for scattering them throughout life?

CHAPTER 10

HANDLE WITH CARE

The Friendship of Ruth and Naomi

All sorts of jokes are told concerning the trouble between mothers-in-law and the spouses of their children. By way of contrast, the story of Ruth and her mother-in-law, Naomi, not only is the recording of a successful relationship between two in-laws but also a true-to-life account of a very deep friendship between two women. Few relationships have ever reached the same height, love, trust, and sheer beauty as the relationship found in this story.

The exact time of the story is unknown, but Ruth 1:1 records that it happened during the days of the judges. Because Ruth was the great-grandmother of King David, the second king of Israel, the time frame of the book of Ruth probably was during the latter half of the period of the judges. It was a time of strife, heartache and bloodshed between Israel and the surrounding nations. We are as uncertain about the book's author as we are the time period, but some attribute it to Samuel.

The little book of Ruth, with only four chapters, is nestled between the books of Judges and First and Second Samuel, which record the story of King David's rise to power and reign. The account establishes the genealogy of Christ, introducing a foreign woman into His ancestral line.

The beginning of the story is set in the small town of Bethlehem in Judah, located about six miles south of Jerusalem on a narrow ledge. The area was surrounded by slopes used for vineyards and orchards. Beyond these slopes were fields where wheat and barley were grown, and beyond the fields were hillsides where shepherds kept their flocks and herds.

In this location lived Elimelech, his wife, Naomi, and their two sons, Mahlon and Chilion. The Bible's description of the family as Ephrathites of Bethlehem, Judah, suggests they were an old, established family in the village.

The Sojourn in Moab

Because a great famine plagued the land, Elimelech and Naomi decided it would be best to leave their homeland and travel across the river to the pagan country of Moab, where the fields were green and the crops were plentiful.

Moab was populated by the descendants of the incestuous relationship between Lot and his eldest daughter (Genesis 19:29-38). The troubles between the countries of Israel and Moab originated during the time when the children of Israel left Egypt and traveled through the land of Moab. The people of Moab refused them bread and water and even hired Balaam to curse them (Deuteronomy 23:3-6; Numbers 22-24). Continued disputes, along with cultural and religious differences, prevented Israel from ever desiring a relationship with the neighboring nation of Moab.

To this pagan country Elimelech and Naomi decided to take their young, unmarried sons. One is made to wonder why they chose to leave Bethlehem when, apparently, most of the other inhabitants stayed during the famine. Why would they want to take their sons to a country where only foreign wives would be available for them? (Marriages to foreigners were condemned in Deuteronomy 7:3 and Ezra 9:12). Evidently, they originally planned to stay only for a short while because Ruth 1:1 states that they "went to sojourn." In the next verse, "they continued there" intimates that their temporary stay was lengthened to one of a more permanent nature.

Elimelech died, probably only a short time after he arrived in Moab. Rather than returning home, Naomi stayed there and her two sons selected two young Moabite women, Ruth and Orpah, as their brides. Within 10 years of arriving in Moab, Naomi found herself not only a widow but also the grieving mother of two dead sons. We are not told how much time elapsed between the deaths of her sons and her decision to leave. In a foreign land, she had lost everything near and dear to her.

When Naomi learned the famine in Judah had ended, she decided to return to Bethlehem. We are not told anything specific about the nature of the relationship Naomi had with her two daughters-in-law. However, the fact that they were willing to leave their native land and their own families leads us to surmise that the three women must have had a better-than-average relationship. Naomi must have been a good mother-in-law.

Understandably, Ruth and Orpah were grief-stricken young widows. Imagine compounding that loss with leaving your country and your way of life, and going with your deceased husband's mother to a country with a strange culture where you no longer could worship the pagan gods of your youth. Everything would be totally different for Ruth and Orpah in Bethlehem. Only a strong relationship with Naomi could have compelled the young women to bid their own families goodbye and begin the long journey to Bethlehem.

As they walked, the three women probably talked about the benefits as well as the problems they no doubt would encounter in Bethlehem. Naomi had been away for 10 years. How many of her former friends and relatives would still be alive? How would they feel about her? Would they hold against her the fact that she had left during the famine? What would the three widows do for an income? The plight of a widow was one of hardship during biblical times.

Despite some natural apprehensions, Naomi's desire to return home remained strong as she walked along the road from Moab to Bethlehem. However, she evidently had second thoughts about the futures of the young widows because she urged them to return to their native land. At the same time, she pronounced a blessing upon them:

> "The Lord deal kindly with you, as ye have dealt with the dead, and with me. The Lord grant you that ye may find rest, each of you in the house of her husband" (Ruth 1:8-9).

The words of Naomi's blessing reveal two significant facts. First, Ruth and Orpah must have been of good character because they had been kind to their husbands and Naomi. Second, Naomi wished each of them might find another husband and have another home.

After expressing her wishes for the young women, Naomi then kissed them farewell. At that time, they did what any normal women would have done in such an emotional situation. Somewhere on the road between Moab and Bethlehem, they stopped and cried.

The strong attachment felt by Ruth and Orpah for Naomi underscored the repeating of their determination to travel to Bethlehem with her: "Surely we will return with thee unto thy people" (Ruth 1:10).

For the second time, Naomi urged her daughters-in-law to return to their native country. She reasoned with them that it was foolish to expect her to produce other sons for them to marry because she was a widow and too old to bear children even if she had another husband. If she were to marry again that very night and conceive more sons, Ruth and Orpah would not want to wait another 20 years for them to mature to manhood.

Again the three women wept, and Orpah, listening to the advice of Naomi, kissed her mother-in-law goodbye again and returned home. After Orpah turned to begin the journey back to her home, Naomi begged Ruth to follow her sister-in-law. (Note that this was the fourth time Naomi urged a return to Moab: Ruth 1:8, 11, 12, 15.)

At this point, in the middle of a lonely crossroad of life, Ruth must have wrestled with a heart-rending decision. Her instinctive longing for home and for everything familiar and comfortable must have tugged at her heartstrings. As her eyes followed the departing figure of Orpah, walking down that dusty road toward home and the grave of a recently buried husband, part of Ruth must have yearned to run after her. She must have felt a certain amount of fear of being rejected in Bethlehem as well as an uncertainty of the future.

Whatever Ruth's natural feelings were, she reached a life-changing decision that day, and at that moment fell from her lips these timeless words of selfless devotion:

"Entreat me not to leave thee, or to return from following af- ter thee: for whither thou goest, I will go; and where thou lodgest, I will lodge: thy people shall be my people, and thy God my God: Where thou diest, will I die, and there will I be buried: the Lord do so to me, and more also, if ought but death part thee and me" (Ruth 1:16-17).

In this passage Ruth made seven promises to Naomi:
1. I will go wherever you go.
2. I will stay wherever you stay.
3. Your people will be my people.
4. Your God will be my God.
5. I will die wherever you die.
6. I will be buried wherever you are buried.
7. Nothing but death will ever part us.

In summary, Ruth vowed she would be with Naomi every step of the way as long as both of them lived.

When Naomi realized Ruth had no intention of returning to Moab, the aged mother-in-law remained silent, and the two steadfast companions continued on their journey toward Bethlehem.

Arriving in Bethlehem

The two weary travelers arrived at their destination in the spring- time at the beginning of the barley harvest, immediately after the Passover. Naturally, the inhabitants of the village gathered around the two women. Naomi must have changed somewhat in appearance during the 10 troublesome years she had been away because they exclaimed, "Is this Naomi?"

Naomi told her lifelong friends no longer to call her Naomi, which is derived from a root word meaning "sweetness" or "pleasantness." Instead, she wished to be known as Mara ("bitterness") because she felt God had dealt very bitterly with her. She had left Bethlehem full only 10 years earlier with a husband and two sons, and now she returned empty. All her family members were dead.

We realize Naomi was using figurative language by the selection of her words "full" and "empty," but we are made to wonder where her sense of gratitude was. Was Naomi justified in her bitterness toward God? Was she not grateful to Him for the measure of health that enabled her to walk home? And had she completely overlooked the unselfish devotion of the young woman who had traveled by her side all the way from Moab and had given up everything near and dear to her just to be with her? Was she not grateful for God's providence in providing her with such a devoted lifetime companion?

The Business of Living

The two women had made their long journey without harm, and now that they were safe in Bethlehem, survival became their top priority. Because Ruth was the younger of the two women, she assumed the responsibility of putting food on the table.

Ruth asked Naomi for permission to glean ears of corn from a nearby field. Because Israel had no welfare or social security system, those who had no other means of making a living were allowed to gather grain left by the reapers in area fields. In fact, a special provision for the needy was made in Leviticus 19:9-10.

Evidently, Ruth had been taught something about the Jewish laws because she was familiar with the custom. The words of Ruth 2:2 indicate that Ruth wished to glean from whatever field was favorable to her. She seemed to know nothing about Boaz at this time. However, she happened to work on a part of the field that belonged to Boaz, who was a wealthy kinsman of Elimelech.

Boaz lived in the town of Bethlehem, but he apparently had the practice of personally overseeing those who worked for him. In fact, he even greeted his workers in the field with a blessing: "The Lord be with you." The simple words of Boaz revealed much about his good name and noble character.

Boaz noticed the strange young woman gleaning in his fields and asked the overseeing servant about her identity. He was told she was the young Moabitish woman who had returned with Naomi.

When Boaz approached Ruth, he told her she could remain in his fields throughout the harvest and that he would provide water and safety for her while she worked. Because she was a stranger in the land, Ruth was overwhelmed by Boaz's kindness and asked him why he had been so good to her. He answered that he had heard about all the good things she had done for Naomi even after Ruth's own husband had died. He also had learned that she had forsaken her people and her homeland to follow Naomi. Her faultless reputation paved the way for Boaz's interest in her. He then asked God's blessing on Ruth "under whose wings thou art come to trust" (Ruth 2:12).

Ruth was thankful for the special consideration she had received from Boaz and expressed her appreciation to him. Boaz then made provisions for her to receive food as she worked. He even told the young men to leave part of the grain they had cut in the field for Ruth to gather.

At the end of that first day, Ruth had gleaned a sizeable amount for her personal harvest. When she returned home and told her mother-in-law about her good fortune, including Boaz's promise to help Ruth throughout both the barley and wheat harvests, Naomi informed her that they were kin to her benefactor. She also urged Ruth to remain in the fields of Boaz.

The Threshing Floor

As the barley season lengthened into the wheat harvest, the relationship between Ruth and Boaz began to grow. Naomi saw an opportunity to make that relationship a permanent one.

Near the end of the harvest season, it was customary for the owner of the land to camp out on the threshing floor to protect the crop from the invading Midianites.

Naomi believed that these conditions were excellent for Ruth to appeal to Boaz to marry her as a kinsman redeemer. Under the Jewish law (Deuteronomy 25:5-10), the nearest kinsman was obligated to marry the widow of his dead relative to produce children on behalf of the deceased, keep the family name for those offspring, and maintain the land and other inheritance intact. This arrangement was called the Levirate Law. ("Levirate" literally means "husband's brother.")

Naomi's question — "My daughter, shall I not seek rest for thee, that it may be well with thee?" (Ruth 3:1) — simply implied that she wanted to help Ruth find a proper husband and have a home of her own.

Naomi advised Ruth to bathe, anoint herself with perfume, and wear attractive clothes. She then told Ruth to wait until Boaz had eaten and fallen asleep before going near him. Under cover of the dark Bethlehem sky, Ruth was told to approach quietly the place where Boaz was sleeping, uncover his feet, and lie down. Ruth's response was, "All that thou sayest unto me I will do" (Ruth 3:5). What trust Ruth displayed in Naomi! Accepting her advice was risking physical harm, rape, or even rejection by Boaz. And yet Ruth had enough confidence in Naomi's judgment to risk her own life.

Ruth followed the instructions of her mother-in-law. Boaz awoke and was startled to find a woman lying at his feet. When he asked who she was, Ruth identified herself and asked him to spread his skirt over her — a symbol of protection — because he was a close relative to Mahlon. This request simply meant that she was asking Boaz to marry her in fulfillment of the Levirate Law.

In following Naomi's advice, Ruth placed herself in jeopardy. However, Boaz was an honorable man. In Ruth 3:10 he commended Ruth for her kindness — which can also be translated as piety — and for the fact that she preferred an older man instead of a younger one. In other words, she could have married a young man, rich or poor; instead, she respected the Word of God enough to follow it in keeping the name and inheritance of her deceased husband from becoming extinct in Israel.

After assuring Ruth that he would fulfill his obligation and commending her for being virtuous, Boaz revealed to her that he was not the nearest blood relative. He told her that the next day he would contact the man who was a closer relative and give him an opportunity to do his duty under the law.

Boaz was just as virtuous as Ruth. Taking advantage of her that night would have been easy, but he did not. Before she left the next morning, he gave her six measures of barley.

When Ruth arrived at the place where she and Naomi were living, she told her everything that had happened the previous night. Knowing Boaz's feelings for Ruth, Naomi wisely predicted that Boaz would have the matter settled before the day was over.

The City Gate

Being an honorable man, Boaz followed the Jewish law the next day after his encounter with Ruth on the threshing floor. He found the man who had a closer kinship to Mahlon than he, and then he called for 10 elders of Bethlehem to sit down, listen to the case, and pronounce judgment on the matter.

It seems that Naomi (and probably Elimelech), in great need of money, had sold the family land. The law stated that it was the obligation of the nearest of kin to purchase the land in order to preserve the inheritance of the family.

When the nameless kinsman agreed to redeem the property, Boaz told him it also would be his obligation to marry Ruth and produce children for the sake of Mahlon's inheritance. Because the kinsman already had a wife and did not want to mar his own inheritance, he gave Boaz legal permission to assume the responsibility.

A strange legal procedure followed in such instances. If the man who had the right of redemption would not take the widow in question as his wife, she was to pull off his shoe and spit in his face as a sign of her disgrace (Deuteronomy 25:5-10). In this case, however, the contemptuous part of the ceremony — Ruth's spitting in the face of the kinsman — was not performed. Because the agreement was an amiable one for everyone involved, the removal of the shoe sealed the legal arrangement between the two men.

The townspeople gave their blessings, adding their good wishes by comparing Ruth to Rachel and Leah. Also offered was the wish that the family would be like Pharez, born to Tamar and Judah, from whom had come the Bethlehemites, the ancestors of Elimelech.

The Happy Ending

Boaz took Ruth as his wife — an act representing far more than a matter of duty as the kinsman of Elimelech. Boaz loved Ruth deeply. And in the course of time, a male child was born to their union.

The women of Bethlehem rejoiced with Naomi upon the birth of Obed because Elimelech's bloodline would continue. They praised Ruth for loving Naomi and even stated that Ruth was better than seven sons. It was the women of the town who suggested the name that Ruth and Boaz gave to their baby: Obed. Later Obed became the father of Jesse, and Jesse became the father of David. What a blessing was the great-grandmother of David!

The story that had begun in tragedy ended in happiness. Ruth and Boaz genuinely seemed to love one another, and Naomi became the nurse of the new baby and had a secure home for the rest of her life. The golden thread of trust in God bound the friendship of Ruth and Naomi together for life.

Conclusion

1. The story of Naomi, Ruth and Orpah is proof that in-laws can be friends.

2. We all need friends to lean upon during times of trouble, but a firm foundation for those friendships must be built before difficult times come our way. Naomi, Ruth and Orpah evidently were close to one another even before they lost their husbands.

3. The commitment we offer to our friends must be one of our own free will. Naomi could not have compelled Ruth and Orpah to travel to Bethlehem with her. They set out on that road because they wanted to do so — not because Naomi had pressured them.

4. We can advise our friends on what we think is best for them, but the choice is theirs to make. Naomi tried to encourage Ruth to return to her homeland four different times, but the decision had to be made by Ruth herself.

5. Regardless of our desires, we must be unselfish with our friends.

6. Our attitude of unselfishness elicits the same response from our friends. Naomi's own unselfishness was, no doubt, instrumental in motivating Ruth's beautiful pledge of devotion and self-denial.

7. When our friends are sometimes submerged in their own emotional turmoil and, consequently, seem ungrateful to us for all we have done for them, we should extend unconditional love in return.

8. We never should hesitate to teach our friends about God — by word and by example — because it's the most important need in their lives. However, they cannot be forced to accept Him. We must never underestimate the power of a living example.

9. The most important contribution we can bring to a friendship is our own character. Ruth is the epitome of this principle.

10. Trust is essential in friendship. Ruth trusted Naomi's knowledge of the law and her good judgment concerning the outcome of the encounter on the threshing floor.

11. Friends look out for the welfare of one another. Naomi wanted Ruth to have her own home and family whether she remained in her homeland or settled in a new country. In return, Ruth honored her relationship with Naomi by providing for her material needs and her emotional need for feeling useful (as the nurse of Obed).

12. Each of us will come to major crossroads in life. Those decisions can change the entire direction of our lives. Some decisions are eternal in nature and should be given our most serious concern.

13. We should be grateful for everything our friends do for us, and we never should hesitate to express our appreciation. Ruth was so grateful to Boaz for allowing her to glean in his fields and for making special provisions available for her that she fell on her face and bowed herself to the ground.

14. Purity always pays. Ruth and Boaz easily could have sinned, but they chose to remain virtuous.

15. The golden thread of trust in God binds fulfilling friendships.

Questions

1. Discuss the background of the book of Ruth. Include the approximate time, conditions under the judges, and the origin of the Moabites.

2. According to Deuteronomy 23:3-6, how had the Moabites treated the Israelites when they came out of Egypt? Discuss the incident of Balak and Balaam (Numbers 22:1-24:25).

3. What were the dangers facing Elimelech and Naomi when they took their sons to a land of pagan people? (Note Deuteronomy 7:3 and Ezra 9:12.) Do some research on the sort of idol worship practiced in Moab.

4. Why do you suppose Ruth and Orpah wanted to leave Moab with Naomi?

5. What two facts are revealed in Naomi's blessing upon Ruth and Orpah (Ruth 1:8-9)?

6. What was Naomi's reasoning in her efforts to get her daughters-in-law to return to Moab (Ruth 1:11-13)? How many times did she urge Ruth to go home (Ruth 1:8, 11, 12, 15)?

7. Try to step into the shoes of Ruth and imagine what her thoughts must have been at this time.

8. Ruth stood at a crossroads in her life on that day. What are some of our own crossroads?

9. What were the implications of Ruth's famous words recorded in Ruth 1:16-17? How do you know she was serious?

10. Do you blame Orpah for returning home? State your reasons.

11. Evidently, Naomi had been a good mother-in-law up to this point. What makes a good mother-in-law?

12. Discuss the idea of making a commitment in friendship. Why are we sometimes hesitant to do so?

13. What was Naomi's response to Ruth's commitment (Ruth 1:18)?

14. When the two women arrived in Bethlehem, why do you suppose Naomi had such negative remarks (Ruth 1:19-21)?

15. What were some ways in which Boaz showed thoughtfulness toward Ruth (Ruth 2:8-16)? What do we learn about him from verses 1 and 4 of that same chapter?

16. What did the law require concerning a woman who had been widowed (Deuteronomy 25:5-10)?

17. Describe Naomi's plan for Ruth in fulfilling this law. Do you think Naomi was encouraging Ruth to put her reputation and even her life in danger? Why did Ruth trust Naomi's judgment?

18. Why did Boaz not fulfill his responsibility as a kinsman right away?

19. What part of the obligation was the near kinsman willing to assume? What part did he reject? Explain the legal procedure (Deuteronomy 25:5-10).

20. What blessings did the women of Bethlehem offer to Naomi when Obed was born?

21. Discuss the lessons for today, adding your own suggestions to the ones presented in this chapter.

CHAPTER 11

The Friendships of Christ

A fter the events surrounding the birth of Christ, little is known about His early years. However, the Scriptures do draw the curtain back a bit and give us a glimpse of the young boy from Nazareth as He accompanied Mary and Joseph on their annual journey from Galilee to Jerusalem to observe of the feast of the Passover. When the rituals were over, the parents started the long trip homeward with relatives and other friends.

They had already traveled an entire day before discovering that 12-year-old Jesus was missing. The writer records in Luke 2:44 that they had supposed their son was somewhere in the crowd of pilgrims from their area. Three days later, after searching among their acquaintances, Mary and Joseph found Jesus in the temple as He talked with the learned men. Because Mary and Joseph did not become concerned until the evening of that first day's journey, we may reasonably assume that Christ grew up as a normal boy with friends and probably was traveling with them along the way.

Have you ever wondered what sorts of friends Jesus had as a boy? Did he romp and play with them? Did he have disagreements with His brothers and sisters?

Approximately 18 years lapse between this glimpse into the early life of Christ and the time when He began His earthly ministry. Following in Joseph's craft, the young carpenter undoubtedly knew most of the people in His hometown. We are left to conjecture concerning His early friends, but the Scriptures abound with information about His companions during the last three years of His life. They may be divided into four categories: acquaintances, casual friends, close friends and best friends.

Acquaintances

After the baptism and temptation of Christ, the Savior traveled the length and breadth of the land as He taught the people. Again and again the Scriptures refer to the multitudes who followed this enigmatic carpenter from Nazareth as He healed the sick, cast out demons, and in many other ways certified His divinity through miraculous events. The rich, the poor, the young, the old, the plotting scribes, the Pharisees and Sadducees — all daily followed Him as He tried to accomplish His mission on this earth. He encountered little children and gathered them into His arms. He had compassion on a widow from Nain, who had just lost her only son, and raised him from the dead. At times the emotional and physical pressures related to the demands of so many people made it necessary for Him to escape by means of a boat on the Sea of Galilee or to withdraw for an entire evening.

Many of these people were supportive. Others were His enemies, who daily tried to trick Him into making incriminating statements. Still others were nameless faces in the crowd and were neutral in their allegiance. Doubtless, many followed because of the sensationalism of a man who could do supernatural feats. These people, generally speaking, were acquaintances — not friends. However, from this large outer circle of people, there emerged some casual friends.

Casual Friends

Nicodemus. At least one Pharisee had an open heart. The third chapter of John relates the incident of Nicodemus' coming to the master teacher by night, asking honest questions concerning His teachings (John 3:1-21). Later this same man defended Christ against the accusations of the Pharisees with the question, "Doth our law judge any man, before it hear him, and know what he doeth?" (John 7:51). Later, after enduring ridicule from fellow Pharisees, Nicodemus is mentioned as the one who brought an expensive gift of spices and joined with Joseph of Arimathea in burying the body of the Savior. Nicodemus emerged from the crowd to ask an honest question and then became a devoted follower who later stood up for Christ and even risked his own life in burying the Savior's body.

Joseph of Arimathea. Joseph was a rich counselor as well as a good, just, honorable and secret disciple who refused to consent to the death of Christ. Begging for the body of such a notorious man and then burying Him in his own new tomb certainly was a dangerous mission. Joseph defended Christ while He was alive and did all that he could to give his Master a decent burial. (See Matthew 27:57-60; Mark 15:42-46; Luke 23:50-53; and John 19:38-42.)

The Women at the Cross. John is the only apostle mentioned as being at the scene of the Crucifixion (John 19:26-27), but each of the gospel writers gives recognition to a group of women who had followed their Savior throughout the land, ministering to His needs.

Faithful to the very end, they were still there at the cross, even though nothing could be done at that time but comfort Him with their presence. Mary Magdalene is mentioned by name by all the writers except Luke, who simply states that a group of women followed Him from Galilee and stood far from the cross. Mary, the mother of Jesus, was among these women. A few names have been passed on to us, but most do not have that distinction. They are just ordinary women who ministered to the Lord and His apostles as the men went about their mission of preaching. Perhaps the women cooked some meals for this band of 13 hungry men or even washed some clothes. They did what they could for Christ and His followers and were faithful to the end. We may not know their names, but in all probability, our Lord called them by name many times. Each stepped out from the larger circle of acquaintances into the realm of casual friends.

Mary Magdalene. Mary Magdalene stands out from the rest of the women at the cross, as three of the gospel writers mention her by name. Luke 8:2 states that Christ cast seven devils from her at an earlier time. This passage also mentions Joanna (the wife of Chuza, Herod's steward), Suzanna and many others as being the recipients of this blessing. These women joined those who accompanied Jesus as He went about the country on His mission and "ministered unto him of their substance." Mary Magdalene was at the cross. She, along with another woman named Mary, sat by the tomb on the first day of the week to anoint the body with sweet spices. It was to Mary Magdalene that Christ appeared and asked why she was weeping. Imagine her excitement as she told the disciples about her encounter!

Close Friends

We have talked about Nicodemus, Joseph of Arimathea, Mary Magdalene, and the other women at the cross. These people, along with others, were drawn from a very large circle of acquaintances into a closer circle of casual friends in the life of Christ.

When our Lord began His earthly ministry at approximately 30 years of age, He selected 12 men who spent most of their time with Him for the next three years as He daily taught eternal truths concerning the kingdom. He then entrusted its propagation to their care when He ascended to heaven. These men walked and talked with Jesus, and they shared many meals together.

Who were these select people whom Christ chose to be His apostles? Passing over the wealthy and influential leaders of the nation, the Master instead selected common laborers. Most of them were fishermen, plying their trade in the region around the Sea of Galilee with little formal education or positions of authority. In Acts 4:13 the high priests later marveled at the boldness of Peter and John because they "perceived that they were unlearned and ignorant men."

Imagine the tension that may have existed in this little band of followers with two men of such divergent positions as Matthew and Simon. Matthew was a tax collector for the Roman government before he left all to follow Jesus. Tax collectors, or publicans, were despised by the Jews because of their unscrupulous methods of securing money for their own gain and because of their association with the Roman government. They often were classified with Gentiles, harlots and sinners. On the opposite side was Simon the

Zealot, a member of the Jewish rebel band that opposed the foreign government and sought to establish once again the divinely appointed line of kings. One is made to wonder about the heated discussions that could have ensued around the fire after the evening meals.

Thomas probably always will be remembered in a negative way: as the doubter. He was just as perplexed as the others at various times during their three-year sojourn with the Master, but this apostle viewed questioning as an avenue to learning. When his inquiries were answered to his satisfaction, doubt was replaced with a deeper commitment. After touching the nail prints in the hands of Christ and thrusting his hand into the wounded side of the risen Lord, Thomas exclaimed, "My Lord and my God!" (John 20:28). Then Thomas knew without a doubt!

Evidently, the apostles had little understanding of the true nature of the kingdom. Believing that it would be an earthly government, they frequently disputed over which one would receive a place of power: "And there was also a strife among them, which of them should be accounted the greatest" (Luke 22:24). The mother of James and John even joined in these discussions, desiring that her two sons would have preeminent positions (Matthew 20:21).

Then there was Judas, the only apostle who was not from the region of Galilee. Having been born in Kerioth, a town located a few miles south of Hebron in southern Judea, Judas probably was different in his accent and undoubtedly in other ways. However, the band of apostles thought enough of him to accept him as their treasurer. Imagine having one of your close friends betray you as Judas turned upon Christ!

As divergent as these men were, and as confused as they were concerning the mission of the Master, Christ nevertheless chose to live in close association with them for three years. At times they loved and had compassion. At other times they were jealous and skeptical. They complained. There were power struggles as they argued among themselves; yet, Jesus accepted them with their personality differences and human flaws as His close friends. He gave them the freedom to be themselves, even when it was painful.

Best Friends

From this circle of close friends, Christ seemed to be closest to Peter, James and John — fishing partners who later were referred to as pillars in the early church in Jerusalem (Galatians 2:9). Their names are found frequently throughout the Gospels as they traveled with Jesus in His teaching, and only these three men were with Him at the scene of the Transfiguration (Mark 9:2). The same three apostles were the only ones whom Christ permitted to enter with Him into the house of Jairus for the healing of his daughter (Luke 8:51).

It was Peter, James and John who accompanied their Lord to the inner parts of the garden and there waited for Him as He poured out His thoughts in anguish to the Father. These three apostles frequently are criticized because they fell asleep while waiting, but Luke gives insight in his account: "And when he rose up from prayer, and was come to his disciples, he found them sleeping for sorrow" (Luke 22:45). Luke, the physician, knew how draining such great stress could be to the body and emotions. Sleep can be almost inevitable as a release at such times.

James and John. The names of the brothers James and John usually are linked. They were called "Boanerges" ("sons of thunder") in Mark 3:17. Evidently, they had quick tempers, which probably prompted their desire to call down fire to consume the Samaritans who refused hospitality to Christ and His followers (Luke 9:51-56). Amazingly enough, John later was known as the apostle of love. Jesus accepted these two men with their basic personalities and gradually smoothed away the rough edges by His daily contact with them. Acts 4:13 states that the priests took knowledge of the fact that Peter and John "had been with Jesus." The only time the Scriptures mention James alone is in reference to his martyrdom in Acts 12:2.

It was John, accompanied by Peter, who found a suitable place and prepared the Passover shortly before the betrayal (Luke 22:8). It was John who leaned upon Jesus at that feast. When the trial of Christ is mentioned, most of us immediately think of Peter and his betrayal; but John also was there and knew the high priest well enough to be admitted into the palace. John is the only apostle who is mentioned, albeit indirectly, as being at the scene of the cross, and Christ entrusted the care of His mother to this disciple whom He loved (John 19:26-27). John outran Peter to the tomb on the morning of the Resurrection but hesitated at the entrance while the impulsive Peter rushed in (John 20:3-8).

James and John are excellent examples of the transforming power of Christ, as their explosive personalities mellowed and they became pillars in the early church.

Peter. Andrew and his brother, Peter, were fishing partners on the Sea of Galilee. It was the seldom-mentioned Andrew who brought Peter to Christ. Most of us can readily identify with Peter, the well-meaning, rash, impulsive fisherman who constantly was putting his foot in his mouth. He meant well, but he was so human!

For nearly three years the master teacher shaped Peter's thinking by word and deed, and the pupil was ready to listen. The following words, which Jesus used in introducing a parable, are especially meaningful: "Simon, I have somewhat to say unto thee. And he saith, Master, say on" (Luke 7:40). Note Peter's respect for the word of the Lord in John 13:4-10 as the apostle submitted to the washing of his feet by Christ. Simon Peter's willingness again is seen in the story of the draught of fishes. Peter believed it would be a waste of time to continue fishing, but Christ's word was supreme: "nevertheless at thy word I will let down the net" (Luke 5:5).

Despite his willingness, Peter was impulsive. At the Transfiguration he was the one who rashly suggested the building of three tabernacles (Matthew 17:1-13). We tend to belittle this apostle and his lack of faith as he unsuccessfully attempted to walk on the water to meet his master (Matthew 14:22-33), but Peter did try while others cried out in fear. Would we have stepped out of that boat?

Peter's personality again is seen in Gethsemane when he foolishly rushed to Jesus' aid by cutting off the ear of the servant of the high priest (John 18:10), but this follower probably meant well and instinctively reacted when the Lord was in danger. All of the apostles but Peter and John deserted Jesus during the trial, and they summoned enough courage to follow their master to the courtyard of the high priest. Despite the fact that Peter earlier had vowed he never would forsake the Lord (Luke 22:33-34), he weakened under the pressure of the moment as he cursed and denied Christ when questioned. Later, as Jesus was being led to another part of the palace, He looked upon Peter. Their eyes met, and the penetration of that divine gaze caused the tender-hearted fisherman to leave the palace and weep bitterly (Luke 22:61-62). The Lord of the second chance had confronted Peter with love, and the penitent fisherman was never quite the same.

Peter's natural eagerness no doubt was responsible for his being one of the first to arrive at the open tomb. This side of the rugged fisherman's personality precipitated his splash into the Sea of Tiberias when Jesus appeared on the shore (John 21:1-14).

Peter became the spokesman for the early church. If he had not been so impulsive and willing to try, he probably never would have been selected to stand before the Jews on the Day of Pentecost and have the courage to say, "Therefore let all the house of Israel know assuredly, that God hath made that same Jesus, whom ye have crucified, both Lord and Christ" (Acts 2:36).

Jesus accepted Peter's impetuousness and channeled this trait into usefulness as a mighty leader in the early church: "Now when they saw the boldness of Peter and John, and perceived that they were unlearned and ignorant men, they marvelled; and they took knowledge of them, that they had been with Jesus" (Acts 4:13).

They had been with Jesus!

Mary, Martha and Lazarus. The little village of Bethany was only about two miles from the bustling city of Jerusalem. In this quiet town, Christ frequently found refuge from the pressure of His work and the taunts of His enemies as He relaxed at the home of His close friends: Lazarus and his two sisters, Mary and Martha. The affection the Lord felt for this family is eloquently, but simply, expressed with the words, "Now Jesus loved Martha, and her sister, and Lazarus" (John 11:5).

The door to this loving home is cracked ajar for three glimpses into its everyday life. On one occasion Jesus had gone there for a meal. Martha, the practical one, was busy preparing the food, and her sister, Mary, was sitting at the feet of Christ, listening to His words concerning spiritual matters rather than helping Martha.

Evidently feeling that she was being treated unfairly, in exasperation Martha blurted, "Lord, dost thou not care that my sister hath left me to serve alone? bid her therefore that she help me" (Luke 10:40). Just as a parent might gently correct a strong-willed child, Jesus chided His friend Martha with these words:

> "Martha, Martha, thou art careful and troubled about many things: But one thing is needful; and Mary hath chosen that good part, which shall not be taken away from her" (Luke 10:41-42).

Someone had to prepare the meal that day, and Martha was performing a worthwhile task. However, her priorities were not in order. Christ accepted the basic personalities of his friends as they were, but He felt close enough to Martha to call attention to her flawed attitude.

The second glimpse into the home of Mary, Martha and Lazarus is of a more somber nature. The sisters sent a message to Jesus with the simple words, "Lord, behold, he whom thou lovest is sick" (John 11:3). Sensing danger from the Jews, the apostles urged their leader not to go into Judea, but His affection for Lazarus was too great: "Our friend Lazarus sleepeth; but I go, that I may awake him out of sleep" (John 11:11). It was the practical, outspoken Martha who met the little band of travelers on the road before they entered the town and chided Jesus for not coming immediately. A short while later, Mary also ran to her friend while He was on the road leading into Bethany with the exact words of Martha: "Lord, if thou hadst been here, my brother had not died" (Luke 11:32).

Lazarus already had been dead four days, his body naturally decomposing, when Jesus ordered the stone to be rolled away from the cave where the body had been placed. Imagine the hushed atmosphere as the friend of Lazarus gave the simple but powerful command, "Lazarus, come forth" (Luke 11:43).

In John 12, after this momentous encounter of Christ with His three friends from Bethany, we are allowed the third glimpse into their home. The occasion was another meal, served six days before the Passover, where we see that the basic personalities of the two women had not changed. Martha was still the one who did the serving, and it was the spiritually minded Mary who anointed the feet of Jesus with expensive ointment and then wiped them with her hair. Judas objected to Mary's behavior with the seemingly noble thought that the ointment could have been sold and given to the poor. Christ scolded Judas by noting that His body had been given an early anointing for His imminent burial and that there would always be poor people deserving of special care.

Christ was divine, but He lived in a physical body with human emotions. He needed a home away from home where he could relax with friends and gain strength to continue His mission. The home of Mary, Martha and Lazarus provided such a refuge. Through its open door we are given a glimpse of the companionships of the Son of God while He lived on this earth.

Conclusion

Thousands of people crossed the path of Jesus. Most were nameless faces in the crowd, and some were enemies who daily plotted to snare Him in some trap. Others adored Him as they paved His way into Jerusalem with palm branches only a week before they angrily demanded, "Crucify him" (Mark 15:13).

Some stepped from the shadows of the crowds to assume a significant place in the life of Jesus: Nicodemus, Joseph of Arimathea, Mary Magdalene and the other women who were at the cross, Mary, Martha and Lazarus, among others.

Probably the most significant lesson we learn from Christ and His friends regards Christ's steadfastness to His mission in life. Because Christ was living in a human body, friends enriched His life. In turn, He Himself enriched the lives of most of His friends. However, His main objective was not to cultivate and influence friends. He came to do the Father's will, and all else was subservient to that aim. He never compromised the truth in order to keep a friend.

We all can take heart from another valuable lesson taught to us by Jesus: When we feel we've been betrayed by our friends, may we ever be mindful of those who deserted the only perfect person who ever walked this earth. One of His close friends betrayed Him and paved the way for His death on the cross. One of His best friends, in the heat of the moment, denied ever even knowing Him. Few of us have ever been so betrayed and mistreated. As our mediator, Christ understands when we take our friendship problems to the Father.

Questions

1. What does the incident of the youthful Christ at the temple reveal about His relationship to His parents? Do you believe Mary and Joseph were negligent in their care of Him since they did not even discover their child was missing until they had traveled a day's journey?

2. Why do you suppose Nicodemus waited until the darkness of night before visiting Jesus? Discuss his conversation with the Master as it is revealed in John 3. According to John 19:38-42, how did Nicodemus endanger his own life by performing one last act of kindness to Jesus?

3. What had the group of women who were present at the cross done for the Lord while He traveled in His earthly ministry? Read the accounts of their services as they are revealed in Matthew 27:55-56; Mark 15:40-41; Luke 23:49; and John 19:25. As Christ no longer walks upon this earth, how can we serve Him now? (See Matthew 25:31-40).

4. Mary Magdalene was in the group of women who stood at the cross and had earlier ministered to Jesus. What had He done for her, according to Luke 8:2? How can a debt of gratitude motivate us to greater service? Discuss the awe and excitement Mary Magdalene must have felt when Jesus talked with her at the tomb (John 20:11-18).

5. Joseph of Arimathea would not give his consent to the death of Christ. What else did he do for Christ? (Note Matthew 27:57-60; Mark 15:42-46; Luke 23:50-53; and John 19:38-42.)

6. Discuss the characteristics of the apostles in relationship to their occupations, their educations, and their temperaments. Give someone the assignment of browsing through the gospel accounts and noting the incidents of disagreements among these followers of Jesus. How do you suppose the Lord must have felt

at the end of most days? Do you think you would have been so longsuffering?

7. Mark 3:14-15 states that Christ selected the apostles to be with Him, preach and perform miracles. Acts 4:13 records the reaction of the religious rulers after they had listened to the preaching of Peter and John. Not only were they amazed at the boldness of such unlearned and ignorant men, but they also "took knowledge of them, that they had been with Jesus." Why was it important for the apostles to be with Jesus? How can we be with Him today?

8. In what ways was Judas different from the other apostles? According to Luke 22:3, Satan entered into Judas about a week before the death of Christ. Earlier Jesus observed that "one of you is a devil" (John 6:70). Did Judas have any control over Satan's entering his body? Trace the steps of Judas on the night before the Crucifixion. Does he ever show remorse?

9. James and John stepped out of the circle of close friends to become best friends with Christ. They were called "Boanerges" ("sons of thunder") in Mark 3:17. The passage in Luke 9:51-56 substantiates the evidence that the brothers had quick tempers. Later John was known as the apostle of love, and James became the first apostle to give his life for the cause of Christ (Acts 12:2). Discuss the transforming power of the Master.

10. Cite examples of Peter's impulsiveness. How did the Lord use this natural characteristic for the furtherance of the kingdom?

11. Contrast the different personalities of Mary and Martha. Relate the three recorded instances of Christ's being in their home. (See Luke 10:38-42; John 11:1-46; and John 12:1-11.) Jesus evidently felt close to Mary, Martha and Lazarus (see John 11:3, 5). Why do we all need close friends?

12. Christ called Lazarus "friend" in John 11:11. He also called Judas "friend" in Matthew 26:50. Do some research into the nuances of the meanings of these two words in the original text. Did Jesus feel the same about the two men?

13. What are the most important lessons you've learned from the study of Christ and His friends?

CHAPTER 12

Troubled Bible Relationships

Troubled relationships have plagued mankind since the dawn of time. As discussed in Chapter 8, friendships with family members have potential for problems. Cain's infuriation with Abel was the spark that ignited the flame of the first murder. Let's take a quick walk through the Scriptures and note the causes of trouble among God's people, as well as the methods used to resolve those conflicts.

Abraham and Lot
(Genesis 13-14; 19)

Lot, the nephew of Abraham, accompanied his uncle at the time of his departure from Ur of the Chaldees. No conflicts were recorded during the time the families were making the journey to Canaan nor during the time spent in Egypt because of the famine. But when the relatives settled in Canaan, a problem arose.

Because both men had large flocks and herds, not enough pasture was available to them if they stayed together. The herdsmen of Abraham and Lot quarreled with one another about the rights to pastures. Abraham's solution was offered in these words: "Let there be no strife, I pray thee, between me and thee, and between my herdmen and thy herdmen; for we be brethren" (Genesis 13:8). When Abraham gave his nephew the first choice of the land, Lot selected the valley of the Jordan River while Abraham kept the hill country.

Later Lot and his family were captured by the kings of the East during a conflict and were rescued by Abraham. Lot then returned to Sodom and its wickedness. When Abraham was told by the three visiting strangers about the imminent destruction of Sodom, he interceded on behalf of Lot and begged that the city be spared if only 10 righteous people could be found. Only four were found, however, and Sodom was destroyed. During the destruction Lot's wife turned into a pillar of salt when she looked back, despite warnings not to do so. Lot and his two daughters then fled to the mountains and spent the remainder of their lives there.

Several biblical principles are found in this incident. First, putting distance between ourselves and those with whom we could have conflict is sometimes best. Second, our motives should be completely unselfish. And third, we always should have the other person's best interest at heart and do whatever we can to help them.

Jacob and Esau
(Genesis 25:19-34; 27:1-28:9; 32:1-33:17)

When Jacob deceived Isaac to receive the blessing of his birthright, Esau was furious and threatened to kill his twin brother. Jacob fled to the house of his uncle Laban at Haran, where he lived for 20 years before returning to his homeland. Because of his own former devious ways, Jacob feared meeting Esau again, so in order to pave the way for better relations, Jacob sent messengers to his brother and asked for his grace. When the messengers returned with the news that Esau had 400 men with him, Jacob was distressed. He then sent large flocks and herds of animals as gifts to the one whom he had wronged, in an effort to mitigate the tension between them.

Fearing the worst, Jacob humbled himself, ran to Esau in penitence and, to his relief, was received with open arms. At first Esau refused the gift of the animals because he already had an abundance, but upon Jacob's urging, Esau finally accepted the gesture of appeasement. Jacob settled in Canaan while Esau took his Canaanite wives, along with all his flocks and herds, and returned to Seir (the region known as Edom).

No two people could have had more hostility between them than these twin brothers, but given some space and time, the two were able to work out their problems peacefully. When the brothers first encountered one another after an absence of many years, their reunion probably would not have been as amicable if Jacob had not offered the gifts of his flocks and herds, along with his sincere penitence, for the wrongs he had committed. The first step needed to be taken, and Jacob stepped forward to make things right.

Joseph and His Brothers
(Genesis 37-50)

When Joseph was about 17 years old, his father, Jacob, had a colorful coat made for his favorite son. The father's partiality, along with Joseph's prophetic dreams, incited the older brothers to throw their younger sibling into a pit and later sell him as a slave to the Ishmaelites, who then carried him to Egypt.

While in this strange land, he was sold to an influential man named Potiphar, whose wicked wife tried to entice the young slave to commit adultery with her. When he refused, she lied about the incident and had him cast into prison. If Joseph had been treated fairly, he should have been released through the influence of Pharaoh's butler, whose dream Joseph interpreted but who forgot to mention the young Joseph to Pharaoh until quite some time had passed.

Many years later, after Joseph had risen to a position of leadership, his brothers unknowingly encountered him when they journeyed to Egypt to buy food to sustain them during the famine. Imagine Joseph's feelings when he first laid eyes on the 10 brothers who had betrayed him in such a ruthless manner. Although Joseph recognized them, they had no idea of his true identity as he now was a grown man, dressed in expensive Egyptian clothes and speaking the language of that nation.

At first Joseph informed them, through an interpreter, that they must be spies and, consequently, would be held as prisoners until one of them journeyed to Canaan and returned with their youngest brother in an effort to prove their motives. After three days of imprisonment, however, the brothers were told that all but one of them could return to Canaan to get young Benjamin.

Talking among themselves, the brothers discussed their predicament in relation to the wrongs they earlier had committed toward Joseph. Overhearing their conversation and realizing their remorse, Joseph turned aside and wept privately. He then returned to his brethren, bound Simeon to be held in prison, and sent the others home.

At first Jacob was reluctant to send Benjamin, his youngest son, to Egypt; he finally relented when the famine again became oppressive. When Joseph once again saw his brothers, he commanded his servants to prepare a great feast. The brothers then bowed and made obeisance. The sight of Benjamin was almost more than Joseph could bear. He excused himself and went into another room to weep. After washing his face and composing himself, he returned to the feast.

Using the ruse of hiding his own silver cup in Benjamin's sack when the brothers departed the next day, Joseph again had all the brothers brought back to him. Judah, who feared that Benjamin would be kept in Egypt as a servant, made a dramatic plea to Joseph to return the young boy to his aging father, who could tolerate no more sorrow after losing his wife and Joseph. Judah himself asked to take the place of Benjamin and remain as a servant.

Joseph was so touched by Judah's devotion and concern for their father that he sent all his servants from the room and weepingly made himself known to his brothers. At first they were troubled over Joseph's revelation, but Joseph relieved them of any guilt as he explained how all things had worked together for good in the divine providence of God. He kissed his brothers, wept with them, and all was made right in their relationship. Joseph then sent them to move Jacob and all their households to a choice place in the land of Egypt.

Several biblical principles emerge from this incident:

1. Even after a heinous crime is committed against someone in a relationship, restoration is possible if both sides are willing to give a little bit.

2. Despite all the horrible things done to Joseph, he was still able to feel deep love for his brothers and was openly willing to express that affection to them.

3. The brothers showed remorse for their wrongs.

4. Joseph relieved his brothers of guilt when he acknowledged that good had come from their evil deeds: "But as for you, ye thought evil against me; but God meant it unto good, to bring to pass, as it is this day, to save much people alive" (Genesis 50:20).

Imagine what the outcome of the story might have been had the Egyptian ruler remained stubbornly defiant. After all, he certainly had been mistreated by 10 wicked brothers and one scheming woman. He also had been slighted because of the human frailties of Pharaoh's chief butler. This son of Jacob had every right to be hurt and angry. Instead, he knew he had a mission in life: to do the will of God. It was that unwavering faith that made it possible for him to remove his glasses of justifiable bitterness and view the entire situation through the forgiving lens of a child of God.

When the one who has been wronged continues to return good for evil, the evildoers are encouraged to repent of their sins. If we are willing to take the first step and outwardly express our love for the other person, the conflict often can be resolved. If, however, both parties remain behind the line drawn in the dust and refuse to give an inch, then the conflict, with all its pain, becomes set in concrete and is always with us as a millstone around our necks.

Joseph, to the best of his ability, always tried to do what was right and left the outcome of the situation in the hands of God. Genesis 50:20, a statement of unwavering faith — "ye thought evil against me; but God meant it unto good" — is again embodied in the words of Romans 8:28: "And we know that all things work together for good to them that love God."

David and Saul
(1 Samuel 16-31)

According to the Scriptures, David's first encounter with King Saul occurred when the ruler was troubled emotionally, and his servants urged him to seek the services of a skilled harpist to sooth him. Evidently, David's reputation as a musician was widespread, as the servants recommended that the youngest son of Jesse be invited to play his harp for Saul. Not only was he an accomplished musician but also valiant, a brave warrior, prudent and handsome, and God was with him (1 Samuel 16:18). This young shepherd from the hills eventually became the king's armor bearer, and Saul loved him greatly. Because David "behaved himself wisely," the king put him in charge of all his soldiers.

As the women openly praised the young hero in the streets, jealousy reared its ugly head and Saul "eyed David from that day and forward." As a result, the king attempted several unsuccessful schemes to take the life of David in the palace area, so God's anointed one fled. He spent the next 10 years literally running for his life throughout the Judean hills while Saul hunted him.

Can you imagine David's feelings during those 10 years of running from Saul? The young shepherd had been anointed by God to assume the leadership of Israel. The position was to be his, and yet David had enough respect for the office and for God's timing to treat King Saul with respect and simply wait.

While David and his men were hidden along the sides of the cave in the rugged wilderness of Engedi, Saul entered, and David's men urged their leader to take advantage of the king's vulnerable position. The fugitive did cut off a part of Saul's robe but later was overcome with remorse because he respected the office of God's anointed king. After both parties had left the cave, David called out to Saul and made him aware of his close encounter with death. When the king heard these words, he wept and acknowledged that David was more righteous than he because David had rewarded evil with good.

Later, in the wilderness of Ziph, David had another opportunity to kill Saul. The king's 3,000 men were asleep when David and his nephew, Abishai, stealthily crept into their camp under cover of darkness. There they found Saul asleep in the trench with his spear stuck in the ground. Abishai believed that God had set up a perfect trap for the destruction of King Saul and begged David for permission to kill him with only one blow from his own spear. But David refused because Saul was still God's anointed one. Taking the spear and Saul's vessel of water, David and Abishai crept back to their own camp where the fugitive called out to the king and informed him of another close encounter with death at his hands. This merciful attitude finally prompted Saul to admit he had sinned, and he promised no more harm. David and King Saul then parted, never to meet again upon this earth. The king left to meet his doom, and David waited for God's appointed time to assume leadership of the kingdom.

King Saul later died in battle with the Philistines on the mountain of Gilboa. His three sons already had been killed when he was wounded, and he begged his armor bearer to end his life, but the request was refused. In desperation, Saul fell on his own sword, and the armor bearer did likewise.

David, rather than rejoicing over the death of someone who had hunted him relentlessly for 10 years, was so overcome with grief that he tore his clothes, mourned, wept and fasted for King Saul, Jonathan, and the entire nation of Israel.

The relationship between David and Saul was never made right. Even after their last encounter, accompanied by all of Saul's promises never to harm the youth, evidently the future king still did not believe the relationship had mended because David said in his heart, "I shall now perish one day by the hand of Saul," and he escaped to the land of the Philistines (1 Samuel 27:1-4).

An important lesson for all of us is found in this story. Regardless of the manner in which Saul treated David, he always respected God's will and tried to do what was right despite his own natural impulses. Saul was penitent on at least two different occasions because David had returned good for evil. If we want to try to change the manner in which people treat us, we must begin by altering our actions toward them.

Although some things may remain unchanged, at least we can know that we have done what is right and can be at peace with ourselves. A few people will never change the way they behave, but we always must be responsible for one thing: our own actions. Doing God's will and trying to keep our thoughts and behavior right in His sight are more important than any hurts or injustices we may receive. With the help of God, we can rise above the pain.

Christ and the Apostles

Because Christ was living in a human body, we are made to wonder whether or not He ever became discouraged. For three years the Master's band of apostles followed Him from place to place, sharing meals with Him, watching Him perform miracles, and listening to His messages. Yet, they argued among themselves concerning their rank in the kingdom, and even at the time of the Crucifixion, they still had no real understanding of the spiritual nature of the kingdom.

Despite their close association with Jesus, the apostles sometimes failed as partners in the relationship. Judas, a daily companion for three years, betrayed the Lord into the hands of the authorities. His closest friends deserted Him in the garden. Only Peter and John followed Him to the palace of the high priest where He was tried, and then Peter denied he knew Jesus.

In the end, after daily interaction with His followers for three years, Christ was alone when He was suspended between heaven and earth as He carried the weight of the sins of humanity on His shoulders.

It seems apparent that Jesus was surrounded by people and even had close relationships with a few. Of His three closest friends — Peter, James and John — only Peter and John followed Him to the palace of the high priest. Even Jehovah turned His back on the sacrificial Lamb as He hung from the cross.

Although Christ enjoyed the joys of friendship while He lived in a human body, He did not come to this world to win friends. He had a single mission: to do the Father's will. All else was subservient to that mission.

When we become mesmerized by the values of the world and sometimes feel that earthly friends constitute our passport to happiness, perhaps we should stop and remember that we, too, have a mission in life. We are here to do the will of the Father. All else is secondary. Generally speaking, following the principles of Christianity will enable us to develop the qualities we need to be good friends to others. Despite being the kind of person we should be, however, we also will feel betrayed by some whom we have befriended. We will be frustrated with their human frailties at some time or another. But none of these things should ever cause us to forget that our reason for being on this earth is to glorify God and do His will.

Paul and Barnabas

Few other troubled Bible relationships seem to be as enigmatic as that of Paul and Barnabas. How could two such devoted coworkers in the Lord's kingdom have had such a misunderstanding that they parted to go their separate ways? Let's begin by considering some characteristics of each man before their paths crossed the first time.

Our first contact with Barnabas is during the earliest days of the church. So many of the initial converts were foreign Jews who had traveled to Jerusalem for religious observances where they heard the teaching of the apostles on the Day of Pentecost and were converted to Christianity. Their physical needs were met through the unselfishness of those who had possessions. Scripture tells us that those who had land or houses sold them and laid the money at the feet of the apostles for distribution. In the account related in Acts 4:36-37, Barnabas is the only one whose name is given. (Ananias and Sapphira are mentioned in the next chapter.) Was Barnabas singled out for this honor because of the size of his gift, his position and influence in the early church, or his later companionship with Paul? The Scriptures are silent.

Acts 4:36 states that the interpretation of the name of Barnabas is "son of consolation" (encourager). He was a Levite from the country of Cyprus, a land famous for its crops of figs, oils, wheats and wine. Possession of land in Cyprus was usually tantamount to great prosperity. Our introduction to Barnabas, therefore, informs us that he was a zealous new foreign convert who unselfishly sold what he had to meet a financial crisis in the early church.

Paul's name also is mentioned during the beginning days of Christianity. When Stephen, the first person to give his life for Christ, was put to death, we are told that Saul "was consenting unto his death … he made havoc of the church, entering into every house, and hailing men and women committed them to prison" (Acts 8:1, 3).

Born in the industrious Greek city of Tarsus and taught the trade of making tents as a young Jewish boy, Saul later was sent to

Jerusalem to sit at the feet of the well-known Jewish teacher Gamaliel. This fierce, young Pharisee was unequaled in his zeal for persecuting the early Christians. His opposition to these people even led him to the high priest in Jerusalem to receive official permission to travel as far as Damascus and take Christians, both men and women, bound to Jerusalem.

On the road to Damascus, Saul's life-changing encounter with Christ occurred. After three days of blindness and fasting, he obeyed his Lord in baptism in Damascus at the hands of Ananias. Immediately, Saul began to preach for the cause of Christ in Damascus. In Galatians 1:17-18 we learn from Paul that he spent a long period of time in Arabia after his conversion. After three years he finally ventured to Jerusalem to join the cause of Christ with the disciples there, "but they were all afraid of him, and believed not that he was a disciple" (Acts 9:26).

Try to step into the shoes of the Christians in Jerusalem. The man who once had persecuted the disciples so relentlessly now claimed to be a follower of Christ. Would you have believed him? Would you have invited him into your home? Could you have gone to sleep knowing he was in the same house? Would you have even wanted to be seen with him? On the other hand, if you had been a nonconverted Jew, would you have accepted someone who, reportedly, had turned against the Jewish religion and now called himself a Christian? Saul had become an enemy to both sides.

It was at this point in the lives of Saul and Barnabas that the paths of the two men crossed. Barnabas, the encourager, apparently believed in the man who previously had persecuted the Christians so relentlessly, and he alone extended the hand of fellowship to the despised Saul. He took Saul to the apostles and stood behind his claim of conversion. In effect, Barnabas risked his own reputation among the early Christians by stepping out to befriend the man when all Jerusalem cried out against him. What a debt of gratitude Saul must have felt! Saul's acceptance by Barnabas probably gave Peter the confidence to invite this new disciple into his home for 15 days (Galatians 1:18).

Saul's bold speech and disputations with the Grecians in Jerusalem once more put his life in danger, and the brethren sent him back to his hometown of Tarsus.

The scene next shifted to Antioch of Syria. When the Jerusalem church was first persecuted, the disciples were scattered far and wide. Some settled in Antioch, and many people — both Jews and Greeks — were baptized. The leaders in the Jerusalem church selected Barnabas, "a good man, and full of the Holy Ghost and of faith" (Acts 11:24), to investigate the progress of the church in Antioch.

Evidently, Barnabas believed he needed some help in working with the church in a Gentile environment because he apparently took it upon himself, without instructions from the leaders at Jerusalem, to travel to Tarsus to find Saul. The two men then worked together with the Antioch church for about a year.

When it was prophesied that a famine would affect the world, the disciples at Antioch gave "every man according to his ability" and sent the relief money to Judea by the hands of Barnabas and Saul.

It was during this period of time when we are introduced to John Mark, who would play a significant part in the lives of Saul and Barnabas. A great persecution arose against the church in Jerusalem, and Peter was imprisoned. After his miraculous freeing by the hand of an angel, Peter went to the home of Mary, the mother of John Mark. (Paul tells us in Colossians 4:10 that John Mark's mother was a sister to Barnabas.) Rhoda answered Peter's first knock but neglected to admit him.

Peter later went to Caesarea while Saul and Barnabas returned to Antioch after completing their relief mission to Jerusalem, taking John Mark, the nephew of Barnabas, with them. It was at this point that the Holy Ghost directed the disciples to send Saul and Barnabas on their first missionary journey, and John Mark accompanied them. On this trip to convert the Gentiles, Saul's name was first referred to as Paul (Acts 13:9).

The three men traveled to Paphos, where they encountered Elymas the sorcerer, who unsuccessfully tried to thwart their evangelistic efforts. From there Paul, Barnabas and John Mark went to Perga in Pamphylia where, for no recorded reason, John Mark left them and returned to Jerusalem. Paul and Barnabas then continued their journey as they tried to evangelize the Gentile world, and Acts 13 and 14 record the highlights of their success.

Not all was glory, however. The Jews at Antioch of Pisidia were jealous of the two preachers and stirred up the people, causing the men of God to be expelled from their coasts. They also suffered persecution at Iconium and traveled to Lystra and Derbe, cities of Lycaonia. At Lystra, Paul and Barnabas were exalted as gods, only later to be persecuted when the Jews from Antioch and Iconium arrived and caused trouble. Paul was even stoned and left outside the city. After leaving Lystra the two missionaries preached in many other places before returning to Antioch of Syria, where they stayed for quite some time.

Trouble reared its ugly head again when some antagonizing Jews from Judea traveled to the Antioch church and taught that the Gentile converts had to be circumcised. Paul and Barnabas "had no small dissension and disputation with them" (Acts 15:2). The church selected these two courageous coworkers, along with others, to obtain the advice of the apostles and elders in Jerusalem.

At this meeting Peter spoke first. He argued that, since God had decreed that the Gospel also should be preached to the Gentiles, the additional yoke of circumcision should not be placed upon them. Paul and Barnabas spoke next, affirming that God was with them in their work among the Gentiles through the working of miracles and wonders. James then suggested that the required Jewish restrictions were to be abstinences "from pollutions of idols, and from fornication, and from things strangled, and from blood" (Acts 15:20).

Paul and Barnabas, along with Judas and Silas, were sent to Antioch of Syria with a letter from the Jerusalem leaders telling them what to require of the Gentile converts. Later Silas decided to remain in Antioch to preach the Word, along with Paul and Barnabas.

Later, when Paul urged Barnabas to accompany him on a second missionary journey to visit and strengthen the new converts made on the first journey, the two men had a sharp disagreement. Barnabas wanted to take his nephew John Mark with them once again, but Paul did not think the idea was wise because John Mark had left them at Pamphylia on the first journey to return to Jerusalem. The contention between them was so sharp that this mighty team in the Lord's service was split, with Barnabas and John Mark sailing to Cyprus while the newly formed partnership of Paul and Silas set out to travel throughout Syria and Cilicia. At Lystra they found the young disciple Timothy, whom they selected to accompany them on their journey.

Paul and Barnabas, who had worked together so effectively for a long time in the history of the early church, went their separate ways because of the dispute over John Mark. Did the two men ever join hands again to teach the Gospel? The Scriptures are silent, and we are left to assume they probably did not.

Why was the dissension so sharp? After John Mark left Paul and Barnabas at Perga in Pamphylia on the first journey, the two men continued with their travels. They sailed on the same boat, ate their meals together, were unified in their preaching, jointly suffered great persecution, were instrumental in settling doctrinal disputes, and in every other way were agreeable and powerful partners in the kingdom. Why did these men not have enough patience and wisdom to settle their disagreements over the advisability of taking the young man with them on a second journey? The Scriptures give no information concerning many of the details, but consider these points:

We are not told the reason for John Mark's departure. Was it legitimate? Did he become ill? Was he simply homesick? Were the rigors of traveling too much for him? Had he become discouraged because of the opposition they met when they encountered Elymas? Did he have a personality conflict with Paul? Was he slack in carrying out his obligations? The answers to these questions could have a bearing on the disagreement.

The personalities of Paul and Barnabas were completely different. Paul was much more aggressive than Barnabas, and he saw matters as being either black or white with little toleration for the gray areas. Before Paul's conversion, his attitude was to search diligently for Christians and put them in jail, even killing them when necessary. After his baptism he was just as forceful in defending the cause of Christ: "And he spake boldly in the name of the Lord Jesus, and disputed against the Grecians" (Acts 9:29).

Nothing could hinder this courageous apostle: "Who shall separate us from the love of Christ? shall tribulation, or distress, or persecution, or famine, or nakedness, or peril, or sword?" (Romans 8:35). Paul gave 100 percent to everything he did and probably had little toleration for half-hearted efforts.

Barnabas, on the other hand, was a mediator. When everyone else was against Paul after his conversion, it was Barnabas who urged the disciples at Jerusalem to give the new convert a chance to prove his new allegiance. Would Peter have kept Paul in his home for 15 days (Galatians 1:18) if Barnabas had not believed in the potential of this former persecutor of the Christians? Would the Jerusalem Christians ever have accepted Paul had it not been for the intercession of Barnabas?

Barnabas and John Mark had blood ties, but the conciliatory trait of Barnabas also probably was instrumental in his pleas for giving his nephew a second chance. Would John Mark have been faithful to the cause of Christ if he had been rejected by his uncle Barnabas as well as Paul? Who knows?

Paul, the apostle to the Gentiles, confronted Peter, the apostle to the Jews, face to face at Antioch regarding Peter's inconsistency in eating with the Gentile brethren (Galatians 2:11-14). Some Jewish Christians from James in Jerusalem arrived in Antioch, and Peter, fearing the condemnation of those Jews, abandoned his practice of sharing meals with the Gentiles. His action influenced other Jewish Christians, and they also acted hypocritically by withdrawing their association. Even Barnabas, despite his years of laboring by Paul's side in converting the Gentiles, joined Peter and the other Jews in their hypocrisy. Could this ambivalence of Barnabas have been a subtle bit of annoyance to Paul? Could it have later added fuel to the fire when they differed over John Mark?

Paul and John Mark were reconciled. Paul was in prison near the end of his ministry when he asked Timothy to come to him and also bring John Mark "for he is profitable to me for the ministry" (2 Timothy 4:11). Evidently, all the differences between Paul and the nephew of Barnabas had been resolved at that point, and they were in full harmony with one another. In Paul's final greetings to the Colossians, he urged them to receive John Mark and even referred to him (along with several others) as being a fellow worker who had been a comfort to him (Colossians 4:10-11).

Paul and John Mark reconciled their differences. Did Paul and Barnabas ever work together again? The Bible is silent.

How the dispute was handled. Probably the most important lesson to be learned from the disagreement of Paul and Barnabas is the manner in which they handled their dispute, which was not a matter of right or wrong but rather one of opinion and judgment. Although their contention was sharp, they simply parted and went their separate ways. We should profit from their example today as we handle our differences of opinion.

Conclusion

After a careful study of several Bible passages, these guidelines for dealing with troubled relationships emerge:

1. Whenever a problem exists in a relationship, we first should look within our own hearts for a possible reason for the dissension.

2. Sometimes putting distance between ourselves and the one with whom we could have conflict is best.

3. We always should have the other person's best interest at heart and do whatever we can to help her. We should love her, regardless of her wrongs.

4. Someone must take the first step toward reconciliation.

5. In matters of opinion, the restoration of a friendship often is possible if both people are willing to give a little bit.

6. We should look for the good — including the providence of God — in any situation.

7. Doing the will of God should be our mission in life and is more important than anything else.

Questions

1. What was the problem that developed between Abraham and Lot (Genesis 13:1-7)?

2. Abraham showed his continued concern for Lot by coming to his aid in what two ways, according to Genesis 14:1-16 and Genesis 18:16-33?

3. What biblical principles for handling problems of this sort can be drawn from these incidents?

4. Discuss the development of the troubles between Jacob and Esau. Do you believe the dispute could have been settled if one of the brothers had not taken the first step?

5. What terrible things did Joseph's brothers do to him (Genesis 37:12-36)? What had Joseph done to spark their envy (Genesis 37:3-11)? Were the brothers justified in what they did?

6. Discuss the high points of the drama that unfolded in Egypt as the men tried to obtain food during the famine (Genesis 42:1-47:28).

7. How does the story of Joseph demonstrate that restoration can be possible? Can the resolution be one-sided?

8. Joseph showed affection for his brothers. Do you believe his display of that love was instrumental in solving the problem?

9. Discuss Joseph's forgiving spirit as revealed in Genesis 45:7-8.

10. Joseph had been mistreated by 10 wicked brothers, one scheming woman, and a negligent butler. How could Joseph say, "but God meant it unto good" (Genesis 50:20)? Relate the biblical principle found in this verse to Romans 8:28.

11. Give the highlights of David's 10 years of fleeing from King Saul.

12. On two occasions David had an opportunity to take the life of King Saul. One incident was in the wilderness of Engedi (1 Samuel 24:1-22), and the other was in the wilderness of Ziph (1 Samuel 26:1-25). What effect did David's goodness have upon the king?

13. If we want to try to change the manner in which people treat us, we must begin by altering our actions toward them. Do you agree or disagree with this statement?

14. How does the story of David and King Saul reinforce the principle that doing the will of God is more important than any hurts or injustices we may receive?

15. Discuss the injustices Christ suffered at the hands of some of His friends. How did He react? His mission in life was not to make friends. What was it?

16. At what point in the lives of Paul and Barnabas did their paths first cross (see Acts 9:26-27)? How important was Barnabas' treatment of Paul in influencing his acceptance by the disciples in Jerusalem?

17. Give the high points of the cooperative work of Paul and Barnabas. After enduring so much together, how could they disagree so strongly concerning the advisability of taking John Mark with them on a second missionary journey (Acts 15:36-41)?

18. Paul was the aggressive one with little tolerance for the gray areas. Barnabas was the mediator, the encourager. What part could their personalities have played in their conflict?

19. What is the most important lesson to be learned from the disagreement between Paul and Barnabas?

CHAPTER 13

HANDLE WITH CARE

Today's Troubled Friendships

E ach of us encounters thousands of people in a lifetime. We immediately are attracted to some of them and repelled by others, realizing that to try to deepen relationships with those whose personality chemistry does not harmonize with our own is a waste of time. We simply don't mesh with all people.

It has been said that some seem to have the knack of evoking the best in us while others arouse the beast in us. The same people who hold no attraction to us probably get along well with many others; in fact, we may have some of the same friends in common. There's just no bond there between us.

We naturally gravitate toward those who stimulate whatever is noble inside our hearts. Even those people whose personalities attract us to pursue deeper friendships with them are composites of traits we share in common — as well as enough differences to keep the relationships stimulating. Life would be remarkably dull if we were all alike. Those differences, however, often cause stumbling blocks in the relationship if we are not mature. Two people cannot remain friends unless they are willing to overlook many little quirks in one another's personalities. We simply react to life differently. If we can laugh honestly over many of our peculiarities, the friendship will be richer because of the diversity.

Relationships that are truly troubled present a different set of problems than those that simply require slight adjustments. Wouldn't it be wonderful if we could do all the right things to initiate and nurture friendships and then live happily ever after, surrounded by a host of loving, caring friends by our side? Life, however, usually does not prove to be a fairy-tale experience. Some bumps appear on the road of anyone's life, and we should not be discouraged when we hit a few of them because doing so is perfectly normal.

The binding relationship of marriage is fortified by the protective walls of spoken and written commitments to remain with one another through thick and thin, through times when we love ecstatically and can see no wrong in anything our partner does, as well as through those days when we do not even like our mates. Because we are committed to our marriages, we work our way through the maze of daily vexations until we have built a rockbed foundation that can withstand even the most violent storms.

Ordinary friendships, however, do not have the security of a marriage covenant. In fact, it has been said that they can be as fragile as a butterfly's wings. Two people have the same freedom to go their separate ways as they had to bond in friendship in the first place. A thoughtless word or an unkind remark can drive a wedge between lifelong friends. The only biblical friendship that was cemented by a formal covenant was that of David and Jonathan (1 Samuel 18:3; 20:12-17, 42).

The Natural Death of Friendships

Have you ever browsed through your high school or college yearbook and wondered what on earth ever happened to some of your former classmates? You worked on class projects with them, attended ball games, sat up talking until the late hours in the dorm sharing your dreams and hopes for the future, double-dated together, and jointly engaged in many activities for several years. When you exchanged your caps and gowns for the grown-up clothes of the adult workplace, your paths widened as you established your own homes and went your separate ways. For quite awhile you exchanged

Christmas and birthday cards, called one another fairly regularly, and even met for lunch or dinner when you were in the same locality.

As the years passed, however, the telephone calls became further apart. You never seemed to find time for lunch or dinner together. The Christmas cards became infrequent and finally ceased altogether. Now you don't even have those names in your address book, and you have no way of knowing how to get in touch with the people who once were a very vital part of your life.

The same scenario is repeated in many different situations. Do you remember some of your first couple friends? You cooked out regularly at one another's homes, enjoyed attending ball games, or even vacationed together. Your children were almost as close as cousins because they also were together as the families shared happy and sad times together. Then perhaps a change of jobs meant moving to another state for one of the families. Your intentions were good as you promised to stay in touch, but gradually the flames of friendship burned to an ember that only radiated memories of happy days of the past.

The scene is repeated over and over with fellow members of a club, coworkers in the business world, sporting companions, parents of our children's friends, community committee members, and dozens of other situations in which our lives merged. We were good friends as long as we were together, but the relationships gradually died when our lives no longer met on the normal pathways of life.

If you are like most people, you probably have kept only a handful of those friendships from earlier times. The cream usually rises to the top, and you have nurtured and maintained only a small number of such relationships down through the years.

What happened to the others? No arguments were fought. No ruptures in the friendships developed. They simply experienced a natural death because not enough nourishment was given to continue their growth. If we had remained in our same original situations, we probably would still be good friends with many of those people today, but nurturing requires time and an investment of ourselves. Friendship requires two willing people. Most of us live life in the fast lane and do not make the necessary effort to maintain long-distance relationships. We could say that many friendships die simply because we move away from one another physically.

At other times we may stay in the same locality, but we move from one another emotionally. The death of these friendships revolves around the fact that we ourselves do not always remain the same. As we experience life and increase our mental horizons, we may change for better or for worse. While the basic core of our personalities always exists, we expand it or allow the vicissitudes of life to take their toll in erosion. Those qualities that attracted us perhaps 30 years ago may have no real interest to either of us now because our goals and our interests in life have changed. Perhaps even a conflict of morals has developed over time. No friendship is worth abandoning one's principles of right and wrong.

In summary, there is nothing wrong with the natural death of some friendships. If we had nurtured them, many would still be thriving. But we didn't. Instead, we moved apart physically or emotionally. Rather than feel guilt concerning their neglect, we simply should try to remember the good things those relationships brought into our lives and always carry those nuggets of gold close to our hearts.

Injured Relationships

Some friendships fail, not because of natural causes but because they have experienced discord and need mending. After all, ruptures can happen quickly. One person can take exception to something the other has said, and a quarrel erupts. At other times, hurt feelings may hide behind the veil of silence. Those feelings may smolder, however, and later erupt into a violent confrontation. Or there may be no confrontation — just an unresolved, slowly eroding bitterness that poisons the joy of the relationship.

Sooner or later, most of us probably will be hurt by friends. Most deep friendships experience trying times at some point. The closer the association, the greater the need for ventilation because the closeness of the relationship can be conducive to irritations. Our superficial friendships normally do not have this problem to the same degree for two reasons: We are not together as often, and we can shrug it off much more easily if our lives are not so deeply involved.

Two Questions

Before confronting a friend, you should ask yourself two important questions:

Is sin involved in this misunderstanding? If you have sinned or if your friend has sinned, as a Christian you have a responsibility in both situations. If you do not talk with her, either she or you could be lost eternally. Under these circumstances you would be a poor friend if you did not care enough to discuss the problem.

> "Therefore if thou bring thy gift to the altar, and there rememberest that thy brother hath ought against thee; Leave there thy gift before the altar, and go thy way; first be reconciled to thy brother, and then come and offer thy gift" (Matthew 5:23-24).

> "Moreover if thy brother shall trespass against thee, go and tell him his fault between thee and him alone: if he shall hear thee, thou hast gained thy brother. But if he will not hear thee, then take with thee one or two more, that in the mouth of two or three witnesses every word may be established. And if he shall neglect to hear them, tell it unto the church: but if he neglect to hear the church, let him be unto thee as an heathen man and a publican" (Matthew 18:15-17).

Is the problem simply one of hurt feelings rather than sin? Perhaps it would be best to think the matter over and analyze your own attitudes. You yourself may need an ego adjustment. Sometimes we simply should demonstrate maturity, realizing that our friends intended no harm by what they said or did. Perhaps you were the one who got up on the wrong side of the bed that morning, and you should overlook the whole incident instead of making a mountain out of a molehill. If your friend embarrasses or criticizes you, perhaps it was her turn to get up on the wrong side of the bed that day and you should be mature enough to overlook the matter. Remember that true love is not easily provoked (1 Corinthians 13:5).

Guidelines for Discussion

Both time and effort are necessary to repair a troubled friendship, but discussion often is required if the infected wound is to be cleansed to allow for proper healing. Otherwise, the damage may be irreparable. Christians are to be peacemakers (Matthew 5:9).

Peace is not necessarily the absence of conflicts but the resolution of those problems. Because confrontations can be unpleasant, we sometimes avoid them as long as possible. Most people hesitate to ripple the water, and none of us likes to admit to wrongdoing. Our egos sometimes prevent our own acceptance of fault, and we can conjure all sorts of reasons to blame the trouble on the other person. Solomon realized the difficulty of reconciliation when he wrote, "A brother offended is harder to be won than a strong city: and their contentions are like the bars of a castle" (Proverbs 18:19).

The same writer also observed, "He that handleth a matter wisely shall find good" (Proverbs 16:20). Most of the time disagreements can be resolved if only we will take the time to approach the other person properly:

Take an honest look at ourselves. Perhaps we are unaware of our own annoying traits. If we are honest, rather than accusing our friend of a slight, we may need to apologize for our thoughtless mannerisms that evoked her unkind words.

Get to the root of the conflict. Before talking with our friend, we should try to get to the base of the conflict. Sometimes we think we are upset for a noble reason when something else is the culprit.

Do not delay a discussion. Ephesians 4:26 stresses the importance of resolving a matter before it has time to fester. Procrastination usually encourages buildup of the harmful, smoldering embers of bitterness. Quite often, allowing for a little cooling off and rethinking time is best before discussion of the problem. However, if a compelling reason to talk over the matter exists, we should not delay.

Approach the other person with the right attitude. Most people can be reached if only we use the right door. Rather than being hostile, we should be willing to accept any blame on our part and ask forgiveness. If they have offended us, we should tell them about it in a nonthreatening manner as we speak the truth in love (Ephesians 4:15).

Talk in private rather than in the presence of others. We all love to hear praise in public, but not criticism. A freer flow of thoughts and ideas is possible when two people sit down together to discuss their problems.

Concentrate on one issue. Do not get sidetracked. This is not the time to counterattack. For example, a conversation between troubled roommates about an untruth that one has spread should not be the occasion to broach the subject of dirty clothes being piled on the floor.

Choose words wisely. Compliment as well as criticize. The tone and inflection of the voice mean just as much as words. "He that is slow to anger is better than the mighty; and he that ruleth his spirit than he that taketh a city" (Proverbs 16:32).

Voices should be kept lowered. Emotions can become escalated if we do not remain in control. "A soft answer turneth away wrath: but grievous words stir up anger" (Proverbs 15:1).

Do not make blanket statements. A confrontation is no place for the words "you always" or "you never." These expressions are prone to stir up resentment because they are seldom true.

Talk honestly. We should be open about our hurts and able to say, "I felt that you were insensitive, and it really hurt me." We should feel unthreatened in asking why the person did a certain thing. On the other hand, our friend should have her turn in expressing her own honest feelings. We should be just as eager to listen to her complaints about us as we are to voice our own. Remember, a germ of truth may very well be found in her criticisms that could make us better people if we will only listen.

Pray together as well as individually. In addition to our own private prayers, both before and after a confrontation, we experience a healing in joining hands and taking our disagreements to the throne of God together, asking for His help in resolving the conflict and in ridding ourselves of any bitterness. We should ask God's forgiveness for any wrongs we have done as well as for the hurt and pain we have caused one another.

Do not expect immediate results. Time has a way of healing if the infection has had the proper treatment. Confrontation may seem intimidating, but it is better than long-term bitterness. Internalized anger is destructive. How wonderful it can be to get everything out in the open as we talk honestly about our feelings!

Sometimes a matter can be resolved immediately, and the friendship can become even stronger because of the openness. On the other hand, time often is required for trust to rebuild. Sadly, sometimes the bent wire never quite returns to its original shape.

An Old Testament Example of Confrontation

Although the relationship between King David and Nathan probably was not one of close friendship, it nevertheless contains some excellent lessons concerning the proper way to help another person see his own error.

David was not always deserving of emulation. At times his actions were deplorable — most notably, his sin with Bathsheba. In 2 Samuel 12, God's spokesman Nathan confronts the king about his sin. Note these highlights of their encounter:

• Nathan went directly to David rather than criticizing the king behind his back and spreading stories about him.

• Rather than relying on rumors, Nathan was certain of the facts before he approached David.

• Nathan selected his words wisely. Rather than criticizing David for his wrongs, he clothed his remarks in the form of a story concerning two men, one rich and one poor, and the slaying of the poor man's one little ewe lamb.

Nathan's approach went straight to David's heart, and the king pronounced his own curse: "As the Lord liveth, the man that hath done this thing shall surely die" (2 Samuel 12:5).

• Nathan spoke boldly. His strategy of using a supposed story to make his point evoked the response he wanted from David. The problem necessitated a brave person to stand before the king of Israel and proclaim, "Thou art the man" (2 Samuel 12:7). After all, King David had the power to take Nathan's life.

• After Nathan pronounced the king's punishment, David acknowledged his sin against God. Nathan then told him of God's forgiveness: "The Lord also hath put away thy sin; thou shalt not die" (2 Samuel 12:13).

• Evidently, Nathan did not hold a grudge against the king. When Solomon, the second child of David and Bathsheba, was born, Nathan gave him a special name: Jedidiah, which meant "beloved of the Lord" (2 Samuel 12:25).

We all could profit from lessons gleaned from this confrontation.

Forgiveness

When a conflict occurs between friends and the matter has been handled in the proper manner, all wrongs should be forgiven. We accept the fact that we are forgiven as we forgive others (Matthew 6:12), but often it is easier to forgive intellectually than to let go of the hurt emotionally.

How many times do we hold on to the pain, rehearsing it over and over in our minds until it eats at the core of our lives as a relentless cancer? If we do not let go, we become the other person's slave. The memory of their wrong continues with us during every waking minute and everywhere we go. Sooner or later, we must release its hold on us. As God has forgiven the offense and remembers it no more, so should we. Probably none of our friends has ever treated us as shamefully as did Peter when he denied Christ at the scene of the trial; yet, the sins of the impulsive fisherman were forgiven and forgotten. This forgiveness enabled Peter to stand before the crowd 50 days later on Pentecost as the Lord's spokesman.

Sometimes the hurt from a wounded friendship is so deep that we cannot handle it alone. We then must acknowledge our inadequacy and rely upon God for strength to do what we know we must do.

Difficult People

In this chapter we previously have discussed the handling of two types of troubled friendships: those that atrophy and succumb to a natural death and those that require confrontation.

The first type of troubled friendship fades away because of a lack of nourishment, not because either person has done anything wrong.

The circumstances of life simply encouraged their paths to go in different directions. If both people had taken the time to nourish the relationship, many still would be thriving today.

The friendships of the second type once were vibrant and alive but have been damaged by an irritation that has come between two people. We must be mature enough to decide whether the trouble is something we should overlook or whether we should confront the friend in order to resolve our differences.

A third group of people falls into a category we shall call difficult people. These individuals are negative, disagreeable, irritable, dominant and abrasive. The problem of relating to people like this is not simply a clash of personalities, as was discussed at the beginning of this chapter. On the contrary, difficult people never seem to live harmoniously with anyone.

Romans 12:18 urges, "If it be possible, as much as lieth in you, live peaceably with all men." Sometimes it's just not possible to live peaceably with some people. We are commanded to love even our enemies (Matthew 5:44), but never are we told to like them!

A time comes when we must accept the fact that some people are emotionally disturbed. They always have been disagreeable and probably will go to their graves angry and irritable. We never should let such people pull us down as they try to draw us into their mode of thinking. As God's children we certainly should never resort to acting in the same manner as they do.

At times we will be unjustly criticized, and people will say unkind things about us. The Scriptures reveal many parallel situations. For example, Stephen certainly did not deserve the treatment he received at the hands of the angry Jews (Acts 7:54-60).

And few have ever encountered more persecution than Jesus. Not only did the mob turn against Him but also some of His own personal friends. Throughout His ordeals, however, He never wavered in these respects:

1. Christ did not allow the behavior of others to influence what He did or change His attitude of love into one of hate. Despite his knowledge that Judas would betray Him, He still washed the feet of that apostle. Peter, one of His closest friends, denied Him. Scripture

tells us that Christ, following Peter's denial, turned to look upon Peter as He was being led from one part of the palace to another (Luke 22:61). Have you ever wondered how much disappointment must have penetrated that gaze?

On the cross Christ still exhibited an attitude of love as He interceded for the forgiveness of those who had betrayed Him. We never should forget that evil is conquered by doing good (Romans 12:21).

2. Jesus never allowed His harsh treatment by others to keep Him from doing His mission. No friendship is ever more important than doing the will of the Father.

An Inward Look

We are wise to examine criticism from others because a germ of truth could well be in their words. It has been said that our friends act as mirrors to our souls. "He that hateth reproof shall die" (Proverbs 15:10).

Asking yourself these questions can help you decide if you, perhaps, have become a difficult person:

1. Are you constantly finding fault with others? Do you seldom have a kind word to say?

2. Do you usually attach an ulterior motive to the actions of others?

3. Do you wear your feelings on your sleeve?

4. Do you overreact to minor annoyances?

5. Are you irritable?

6. Are you intolerant?

7. Do you always seem to be in the midst of a disagreement with someone?

If you answered yes to several of the above questions, perhaps you should turn inward for the solution to your problems.

Conclusion

Because we live in a world of imperfect people, including ourselves, undoubtedly we will experience times in our lives when we have troubled relationships with others.

As Christians we should do our best to resolve these problems in a manner that is pleasing to God. Going to a friend with the right attitude in an open discussion of our differences often can clear the air. We should not allow the conduct of another person to influence our own behavior. Rather than retaliating with our own biting words or gossip, we should return good for evil.

Sometimes restoration efforts are futile, and the friendship is never again the same. Rather than harboring negative feelings, we should pause to remember those qualities that had attracted us as friends in the first place. If we are wise, we will search for these happy memories, place them close to our hearts, and then let the rest go out to sea as a part of the ebb and flow of life. We are composed of bits and pieces of everyone who has ever crossed our paths, and we alone are the ones to determine whether we choose to keep the good or the bad.

It's our decision.

"Forgiveness is the fragrance that the violet sheds on the heel that has crushed it."

QUESTIONS

1. What part do individual personalities play in the attraction of one person to another in friendship? Is this good or bad?
2. How can our personality differences enhance a relationship? How can they be detrimental?
3. Do you believe friendships should involve some sort of a covenant? Discuss the covenant between David and Jonathan (1 Samuel 18:3; 20:12-17, 42). What are the advantages involved in the marriage covenant or contract?
4. How can friendships die a natural death? Is this bad?
5. How can an unresolved conflict feed the bitterness that poisons the joy of a relationship?
6. What two questions should we ask ourselves before the open discussion of a problem?
7. If a problem with a friend is simply a matter of hurt feelings, what should we do?
8. If the contention is a sin, as Christians we have a dual responsibility. What is it, according to Matthew 5:23-24 and 18:15-17?